SURVEY OF COVENANT HISTORY

SURVEY OF COVENANT HISTORY

A Historical Overview of the Old Testament

Walter R. Roehrs

Publishing House
St. Louis

Copyright © 1989 Concordia Publishing House
3558 S. Jefferson Avenue, St. Louis, MO 63118-3968
Manufactured in the United States of America

Library of Congress Cataloging-in-Publication Data

Roehrs, Walter Robert, 1901–
    Survey of covenant history: a historical overview of the Old Testament/Walter R. Roehrs.
        p.   cm.
    ISBN 0-570-04244-5
    1. Bible. O. T.—History of Biblical events. I. Title.
    BS1197.R57 1989
    221.9'5—dc19   88-23706

1　2　3　4　5　6　7　8　9　10　　98　97　96　95　94　93　92　91　90　89

Contents

Acknowledgments

The kind of Biblical lore contained in this book is known in German theological literature as *Biblekunde*. The incentive to use and develop this format to acquaint the American reader with the basic facts of Old Testament history derives from an outstanding example of this type of publication, *Bibelkunde des Alten Testaments* (2 vol.; Otto Weber, Göttingen, 1947).

I should also like to acknowledge my indebtedness to my wife for her review of my writings and for her constant encouragement to labor on. Thank you, Louise!

WALTER R. ROEHRS

Abbreviations

Old Testament

Gen. — Genesis
Ex. — Exodus
Lev. — Leviticus
Num. — Numbers
Deut. — Deuteronomy
Joshua — Joshua
Judg. — Judges
Ruth — Ruth
1 Sam. — First Samuel
2 Sam. — Second Samuel
1 Kings — First Kings
2 Kings — Second Kings
1 Chron. — First Chronicles
2 Chron. — Second Chronicles
Ezra — Ezra
Neh. — Nehemiah
Esther — Esther
Job — Job
Ps. — Psalms
Prov. — Proverbs
Eccl. — Ecclesiastes
Song of Sol. — Song of Solomon
Is. — Isaiah
Jer. — Jeremiah
Lam. — Lamentations
Ezek. — Ezekiel
Dan. — Daniel
Hos. — Hosea
Joel — Joel
Amos — Amos
Obad. — Obadiah
Jonah — Jonah
Micah — Micah
Nah. — Nahum
Hab. — Habakkuk
Zeph. — Zephaniah
Hag. — Haggai
Zech. — Zechariah
Mal. — Malachi

New Testament

Matt. — Matthew
Mark — Mark
Luke — Luke
John — John
Acts — Acts
Rom. — Romans
1 Cor. — First Corinthians
2 Cor. — Second Corinthians
Gal. — Galatians
Eph. — Ephesians
Phil. — Philippians
Col. — Colossians
1 Thess. — First Thessalonians
2 Thess. — Second Thessalonians
1 Tim. — First Timothy
2 Tim. — Second Timothy
Titus — Titus
Philemon — Philemon
Heb. — Hebrews
James — James
1 Peter — First Peter
2 Peter — Second Peter
1 John — First John
2 John — Second John
3 John — Third John
Jude — Jude
Rev. — Revelation

1. What Is "Covenant History"?

At Mount Sinai God said to the descendants of the patriarchs whom He had delivered from Egypt's house of bondage, "I will walk among you and be your God, and you shall be My people" (Lev. 26:12). This promise was God's covenant in its simplest form. God proclaimed and effected this pact in order to restore His estranged creatures to a blissful communion with Him.

Lest this covenant, a human analogy to divine attributes and acts, be misunderstood to be a contract between equals, He defined its terms in "the Book of the Covenant" (Ex. 24:7). Its contents make clear that sinful sons and daughters of Adam and Eve cannot presume to enter negotiations with their Creator or haggle with Him for a settlement of their revolt against Him. They have nothing to contribute to this partnership but owe everything they derive from it to divine goodness and mercy.

In His covenant with the erstwhile slaves of Pharaoh, God also claimed to be the Lord of history. Whatever was to happen in the lives of individuals, kingdoms, and empires would not come about at the behest of arbitrary deities or some impersonal law of nature but solely at His command. In keeping this promise, the Lord of heaven and earth would so fashion and direct the course of mundane events that they would do His bidding and serve His purpose. Consequently, nothing would prevent Him from carrying out His solemn pledge, "I will never break My covenant with you" (Judg. 2:1).

Covenant history, therefore, is teleological, that is, designed to attain a *telos*, a predetermined end or goal. Isaiah affirms this by exposing the impotence of idols made by human beings and adding the divine declaration, "I am God, . . . declaring the end from the beginning, and from ancient times things that are not yet done" (Is. 46:9–10).

Old Testament history is not merely a period of aimless waiting. It proclaims God's moving toward the goal of redemption for all people through the blood of the new covenant. Every event is fulfillment and simultaneously a promise of greater things to come. From the vantage point of New Testament revelation, the Old Testament consists of a myriad of arrows pointing to the fullness of time when "God sent forth His Son . . . to redeem those who were under the law" (Gal. 4:4–5).

In His sovereign and good pleasure, God used many eons of time, many events, and many nations to fulfill His covenanted promises. For this reason particularly, a survey of Old Testament history will prove helpful for a study of the individual books.

The historical setting of the New Testament is measured in decades; the Old Testament books record a history that spans ages. But it is not world history in the usual sense of the term. It is covenant history or *Heilsgeschichte*—history of salvation. From its beginning it is highly selective in the choice and narration of human history. Nations and peoples that are not bearers of the promise are brushed aside in Genesis by a mere mention of their names and origin. In the first 11 chapters, a direct line through millennia of time is drawn from Adam to Abraham (about 2000 B.C.). The lives of the patriarchs are described with some detail. But even these biographical accounts merely sketch the people's response of faith to the covenant and the patience of God with their weaknesses and shortcomings as bearers of the covenant. Each event supplies the background for the next chapter in the history of salvation.

After the death of the patriarchs and before the story of the covenant nation begins, there is another long lapse of time. Four hundred years pass before the record of events resumes (Ex. 12:40–41).

Just as the story of Israel is not world history in the usual sense of the word, so it is not national history either. Its purpose is not to present a continuous account of the most significant developments of political, social, and economic life. In fact, events of considerable national significance are often passed over in silence (cf. the history of some of the kings of the Northern Kingdom—for example, Omri and Jeroboam II). At times the account only briefly recapitulates and summarizes, making it difficult to reconstruct the course of events (cf. the conquest of Canaan in Joshua and Judges). On the other hand, some incidents of national importance are described in detail (cf. David's personal history).

The reader, therefore, must bear in mind the special nature of these accounts. Selection or omission of material is made on the basis of its significance or lack of it for covenant history. The accounts are true and factual, but they do not include all social, political, and economic events. Thus, Biblical history embraces a series of situations that God brought about as He carried out His covenanted purpose in and through Israel.

Israel's history is more than 10 centuries long. It becomes somewhat complex during the time when Israel became a house divided against itself and for two centuries was ruled by a series of rival kings. The Northern Kingdom (Israel) came to an end in 722 B.C. The scene of activity for the next century and a half is almost entirely in the Southern Kingdom (Judah) and its capital, Jerusalem. After the fall of Jerusalem in 587/586 B.C., 50 years elapse before the next connected story begins: the return from the Babylonian captivity. Even this consists of a selection of more or less isolated happenings. Before the gospels of the New Testament pick up the thread, there are several more intervening centuries, the so-called intertestamental period.

All of this history is correctly called sacred. It describes the persons, the peoples, the movements, and the institutions that God used to fulfill His gracious and holy purpose. This is covenant history.

2. The Other Nations and Peoples

In one sense, Biblical history can be called secular history. The historical bearers of the promise were people of flesh and blood, tainted and tempted by sin. By their selfishness and lack of faith they often made profane what God had designed for holy purposes.

Furthermore, the history of the covenant did not transpire in a vacuum, sealed off from secular contact. Since God's people, like all people, were descended from the common ancestry of Adam and Eve, they all had the same capacity and needs. Even after Israel had been chosen to come out from among the peoples and be separate, they continually were affected for good or evil by almost every other nation of antiquity. Also, when Abraham entered Canaan, he did not find an unpopulated and virgin country. As in Mesopotamia, he was again a sojourner among a conglomeration of peoples with a variety of cultures and history.

Why God chose Abraham as the father of all believers remains a mystery. But we can surmise God's reason for choosing Canaan as the Land of Promise. Through this small country ran the highway of the nations. Exchange of trade, conquest of arms, varieties of culture flowed over this land ridge from all directions and at all times.

The prophet Ezekiel describes the position of Israel in the ancient world as follows: "I have set her [Jerusalem] in the midst of the nations and the countries all around her" (5:5). And in God's providence they contributed in various ways so that salvation is "from the Jews" (John 4:22 RSV).

Covenant history is indeed world history, but "the nations are as a drop in a bucket, and are counted as the small dust on the scales; Look, He [God] lifts up the isles as a very little thing" (Is. 40:15).

Thus, a sketch of the more important nations will be drawn in order to understand the Old Testament and especially the part God assigned to kingdoms and empires in bringing about the "promise which was made to the fathers" (Acts 13:32).

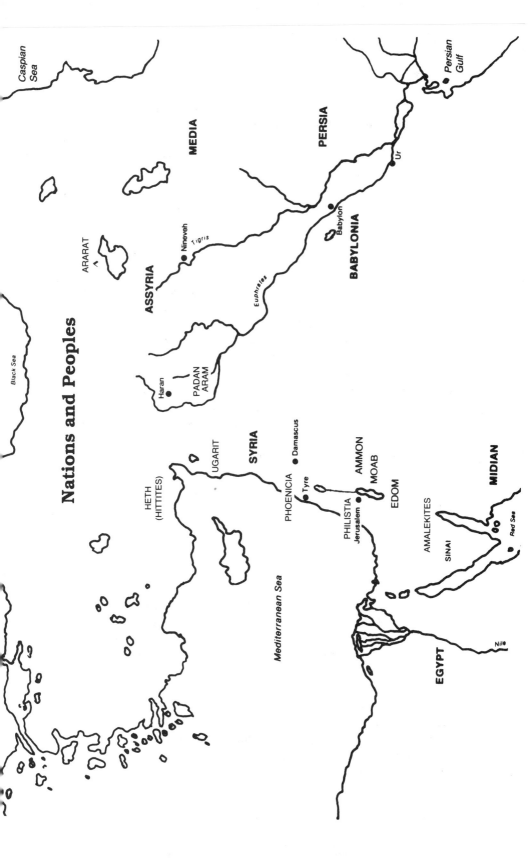

Nations and Peoples

Caspian Sea

Black Sea

MEDIA

PERSIA

Persian Gulf

ARARAT

ASSYRIA

Nineveh

Tigris

Euphrates

Ur

Babylon

BABYLONIA

Haran

PADAN ARAM

HETH (HITTITES)

UGARIT

SYRIA

Damascus

PHOENICIA

Tyre

AMMON

MOAB

PHILISTIA

Jerusalem

EDOM

Mediterranean Sea

AMALEKITES

SINAI

MIDIAN

Red Sea

EGYPT

Nile

Egypt

The land of the Pharaohs played a sustained and at times prominent role in the development of covenant history. From Abraham to the close of the Old Testament, Egypt was on the scene and affected the lot of the bearers of God's promise.

When famine in Canaan brought Abraham to seek relief in Egypt (about 2000 B.C.), he found a land and civilization hoary with age. For a thousand years a Pharaoh had held sway over a united land composed of a previously separate Upper (South) and Lower (North) Egypt.

Late in its history, an Egyptian priest, Manetho (285–246 B.C.), divided Egyptian history into 30 dynasties or successive houses of rulers. At that time the pyramids had been standing for over 20 centuries, having been built during the so-called Old Kingdom (about 2700 to 2200 B.C., the Third to the Sixth Dynasty). Jacob, the grandson of Abraham, came to Egypt after his son Joseph had been elevated to a position of high authority under a Pharaoh who ruled during the period called the Middle Kingdom (12th Dynasty, about 1987 to 1776 B.C.).

When the Biblical record resumes the account of the descendants of Jacob 430 years later, Egypt had experienced some of the most significant developments in its history. Its long period of independence under native rulers had come to an end. Invaders composed of several racial strains came via Canaan. A preponderant element was Semitic. The Egyptians called them *Hyksos* ("rulers of foreign lands").

From their capital, Avaris, in the Delta the Hyksos held sway over Canaan and Egypt for about a century and a half (about 1720 to 1570 B.C.). The offspring of Jacob, probably related to the new masters by race, presumably were left undisturbed. The situation changed drastically when the Hyksos were expelled from Egypt and their possessions in Canaan brought under the control of the 18th Dynasty (about 1570 B.C.). The latter created an empire that extended through Canaan to the Euphrates River. Under the 19th Dynasty (about 1300 B.C.), campaigns of conquest were waged in Canaan for another century.

After this empire period came to an end, Egypt never again became a world power in the Near East. At times, dreams of Egypt's golden age inspired Pharaohs to send armies into Canaan in an attempt to struggle for international power, but its strength was spent. Humanly speaking, David enlarged Israel's borders to an empire status because Egypt could not maintain the power it had during the 18th and 19th dynasties.[1]

The first sporadic attempt on the part of Egypt to reassert its power in Palestine came shortly after the death of Solomon (932 B.C.). Five years after the division of Solomon's kingdom, the founder of the 21st (Libyan) Dynasty, Sheshonk I (called Shishak in 1 Kings 14:25), was able to invade Canaan, partly because of its internal strife. Sheshonk captured cities in the territory of Rehoboam, king of Judah, as well as in that of the Northern Kingdom of Jeroboam (although the latter had sought and found refuge in Egypt before Solomon's death). But Sheshonk's campaign was merely a raid.

At times the Israelites after David were tempted to trust protective alliances with Egypt, but the futility of that hope is graphically expressed by one of the last prophets of Israel: "They [the Egyptians] have been a staff of reed to the house of Israel" (Ezek. 29:6).

No Egyptian army appeared in Palestine for the remainder of the 22d Dynasty or during the weak 23d and 24th Dynasties— about 200 years later. By that time the end of the Northern Kingdom (Israel) was at hand. In a desperate but futile attempt to seek help against the Assyrian conqueror, Israel's last king, Hoshea, "sent messengers to So, king of Egypt" (2 Kings 17:4), perhaps a weak ruler in the Delta area at that time.

The 25th Dynasty made frantic efforts to stem the tide of Assyrian world conquest. Shabaka, the first Pharaoh of these Ethiopian rulers of Egypt (about 711 to 699 B.C.), sent an army into Palestine in 701 to make common cause with King Hezekiah and his confederates in their revolt against Assyrian overlordship. Tirharka, who later became Pharaoh (680–663 B.C.), was probably in command. But he was defeated by Sennacherib of Assyria, and the siege of Jerusalem went on. Some 30 years later, the Assyrians invaded Egypt itself and defeated Tirharka. Thebes, the ancient southern capital of Egypt, was destroyed in 663 B.C.

But Egypt was to intrude once more into the history of the chosen people. When Assyrian control slackened and could no longer be maintained, a native Egyptian dynasty (the 26th, the Saite) established itself and revived the nation's power. The second Pharaoh of this house, Necho (609–594 B.C.), led his armies into Canaan in an attempt to check the expanding conquests of the heir of Assyria's collapsed empire, Babylonia. When King Jo-

---

[1]The reigns of Saul, David, and Solomon coincide approximately with the time of the 21st Dynasty, about 1150 to 930 B.C., when the decline of Egypt had set in fully.

siah refused him passage through the land, Pharaoh Necho defeated Josiah at Megiddo and killed him (2 Kings 23:29–30). Necho then established his headquarters in Syria, deposed the next king of Judah (Jehoahaz), and placed Jehoiakim on the throne. Canaan was once more an Egyptian province—but not for long. Four years later, Necho was fleeing southward through Canaan, defeated and pursued by the Babylonian general Nebuchadnezzar.

Necho's grandson, Apries (Hophra), also unsuccessfully challenged Nebuchadnezzar's claim to Canaan at the time of Zedekiah, the last king of Judah. In spite of prophetic warnings to the contrary, Zedekiah was persuaded by a pro-Egyptian party in Jerusalem to join with Hophra and rebel against Babylonian overlordship. But the Babylonian siege of Jerusalem was merely interrupted long enough to permit Nebuchadnezzar to rout Hophra's army. Jerusalem fell in 587/586 B.C.

Now ancient Egypt was to lose its independence permanently. After 525 B.C. it became a part of the Persian Empire for two centuries. Then in 332 B.C. Alexander added Egypt to his conquests. After his death, it was ruled by the Ptolemies (so named after Ptolemaeus, one of Alexander's generals), until it became a Roman province in 30 B.C.

Philistia

The fertile maritime plain in southwestern Canaan athwart the coastal trade route became the stronghold of an immigrant people who significantly affected the chosen people and existed side by side with them throughout their history. The Biblical account often calls this area "the land of the Philistines" or "Philistia."[2]

The Philistines had come from the eastern Mediterranean coastal areas and islands.[3] Their coming to Canaan was the result of a population upheaval[4] that set in motion the migrations of "the Sea Peoples," as the Egyptians called them. Moving southward, some of these Sea Peoples threatened to overrun Egypt. They were repulsed in a land and sea battle by Rameses III (about 1200

---

[2]The Greek version of the name, "Palestine," later taken over into Latin, eventually came to denote all of Canaan.

[3]Crete (Caphtor) is mentioned specifically in Amos 9:7 and Jer. 47:4. In Ex. 23:31 the Mediterranean is called "the Sea of the Philistines."

[4]The fall of Troy is part of that story.

B.C.[5]) and fell back to the Mediterranean coast of southern Canaan. In an area between Joppa and Gaza (about 50 by 15 miles), they founded a Pentapolis, a federation of five cities: Gaza, Gath, Ashkelon, Ashdod, and Ekron. The leaders, therefore, are called the "five lords of the Philistines" (Joshua 13:3; Judg. 3:3).

In their new environment, their Aegean (Aryan) culture took on a Canaanite-Semitic cast. They assumed Semitic names and adopted the worship of such Canaanite deities as Dagon (as the Israelites also were tempted to do—and sometimes did). Since the Philistines did not practice circumcision, Scripture often refers to them as "the uncircumcised."

Their conflict with Israel began in the days of the judges (Samson, Shamgar) as the Philistines expanded their territory at the expense of Israel. At the time of Samuel (about 1050 B.C.), they destroyed Shiloh, the center of Israel's worship, and captured the Ark of the Covenant (1 Sam. 4). After their victory over Saul at Mount Gilboa, the Philistines were in virtual control of all Canaan. They dominated it from such strategic fortresses as Bethshan, where Saul's corpse was hanged. Saul's son, Eshbaal, forsook all territory west of the Jordan and was forced to establish his headquarters east of the river.

For some unknown reason (perhaps internal strife), the Philistines did not exploit their superiority by reducing Israel to vassalage. As soon as David had united the tribes, he drove out the invaders (2 Sam. 5:17–25) and broke their power by carrying the war into their own territory. (Cf. also 2 Sam. 21:15–22). The Cherethites (Cretans) and Pelethites (Philistines) served him as mercenaries.

Philistine cities continued to exist, though in a semi-independent manner. Judean King Uzziah, for example, found it necessary to break down the walls of Ashdod (2 Chron. 26:6; cf. 2 Kings 18:8) but was not resisted by the other Philistine cities. They are mentioned as separate entities and usually fell prey at later times to the same conquerors that invaded Israel and Judah. The prophets often mention these Philistine cities. Even after the return from the Babylonian exile, Nehemiah (13:23–24) complains that the Jews had married "women of Ashdod, . . . and half of their children spoke the language of Ashdod."

---

[5]In the Biblical record, the Philistines were present in Palestine long before 1200 B.C., for Isaac dealt with them (Gen. 26:1–18). Because extra-Biblical sources shed no light on this, some scholars regard this early reference to the Philistines as a retrojection into the patriarchal age. No doubt they represent an earlier and smaller wave of emigration from the Aegean area.

Phoenicia

Northward along the Mediterranean Sea lay Phoenicia, "the region of Tyre and Sidon" (Matt. 15:21).[6] The Phoenicians spoke a Northwest Semitic language similar to Hebrew and worshiped the gods of the Canaanite pantheon. Hemmed in by the mountains, they took to the sea and established a commercial empire that embraced the Mediterranean. The fabulous wealth that resulted from the maritime trade is described by the prophet Ezekiel (chaps. 26–28). As the middleman in the exchange of various commodities, Phoenicia also developed an alphabet that became the basis for the Greek and ultimately the English alphabets.

Their relationship to the covenant people was generally friendly. David's alliance with Hiram of Tyre continued in effect under Solomon. The Lebanon Mountains furnished the timber for the Jerusalem temple, and skilled Phoenician artisans helped build it. The prophets' denunciations of Tyre and Sidon (e.g., Is. 23; Ezek. 26–28; Amos 1:9–10; Zech. 9:3–4) were based on moral and religious considerations, not political or military threats. One of the most serious of these threats to Israel's faith and way of life came as the result of Ahab's marriage to a Tyrian princess, Jezebel. Baal worship received official status through her influence, and the persecution of the true worshipers of Yahweh is the background for the well-known Elijah stories.

Assyria and Babylon, conquerors of Israel and Judah, also put an end to the independence of the Phoenicians. And Alexander the Great recaptured Tyre in 332 B.C.

Ugarit

Still farther north along the Mediterranean coast, across the sea from the northern tip of Cyprus, lies Ras Shamra, the modern name for ancient Ugarit. We know of no direct relation of this people with Israel. But hundreds of texts discovered there in 1929 and later describe the Canaanite religion with which Israel came into contact in the Promised Land, an enemy that proved deadlier to Israel than foreign armies.

The Ras Shamra texts were found in a library situated between temples dedicated to Baal and Dagon. Written on clay tablets in a cuneiform script of 30 characters, they date from the 14th to the 12th centuries B.C. The language is a Northwest Semitic dialect similar to Phoenician and Hebrew. The literary

---

[6]The territory, dominated by these cities, was called Phoenicia by the Greeks, a term not found in the Old Testament.

forms, both prose and poetry, have a greater similarity to the Old Testament than do those of any other ancient literature.

But the religion of the Ras Shamra texts is as different from the Old Testament as night from day. Building with "stones" taken from the same linguistic and cultural quarry, the Old Testament built a temple of beauty, while the Canaanite religion produced a den of perversion, falsehood, and filth. Of all the religions of the Near East in this period, the cult of Canaan is the most degrading, sensuous, and debilitating. Its devotees richly deserved that "the land vomit" them out (Lev. 18:28; cf. 20:22).

The supreme god of its pantheon was "El," a name used also for God in the Old Testament. El's son, Baal (also a common noun meaning "lord" or "master"), together with the goddesses Anath, Astarte, and Asherah, represent the forces of fertility. Licentious male and female prostitution are the magical rites to guarantee the worshiper that the earth will bring forth crops, animals will produce offspring, and human beings will perpetuate themselves. The sexual excesses had no limits. Even bestiality was a divine prerogative.

This degenerate religion of Canaan, known better from the Ras Shamra texts than from Scripture, also pandered to Israel's lower instincts. Any technique to assure agricultural prosperity proved a great temptation to the Israelites as they settled into an agrarian way of life after 40 years of desert wandering.

Heth (The Hittites)

North of the northeast corner of the Mediterranean Sea, in Asia Minor, lay the kingdom of the Hittites (the children of "Heth" in some translations; cf. Gen. 10:15 and 25:9–10).

The prophet Ezekiel says of Jerusalem, "Your father was an Amorite and your mother a Hittite" (16:3). The story of Abraham mentions the Hittites as one of the many strains that at an early period composed the population of Canaan.[7] Consequently, the Hittites also appear on the lists of the peoples whom Israel was to displace in Palestine (Ex. 3:8; 23:28; etc.) but did not succeed in driving out completely (Judg. 3:5).

Of Indo-European stock, the ancestors of these people had poured out of modern southern Russia as a part of a great *Völkerwanderung* and entered Asia through the territory between the Black and Caspian Seas. In Asia Minor they found a native Hatti

---

[7]E.g., from Ephron the Hittite, Abraham bought the cave of Machpelah for a burial place (Gen. 23:3–20; 25:9–10; 49:29–32).

people and adopted their name. About 1900 B.C. they had established a strong kingdom at Boghazköy at the bend of the Halys River. In about 1500 their forces invaded the Tigris-Euphrates Valley and even destroyed Babylon. There is no reason why these new immigrants could not have also penetrated Canaan in considerable numbers. To what extent they were semitized cannot be ascertained. Hebrew names such as Ephron (Gen. 23:10), Ahimelech (1 Sam. 26:6), and Uriah (2 Sam. 11:3) would indicate that they were adaptable to their new environments.

After about 1650 B.C. this first period of strength came to an end. But from 1400 to 1200 we see a resurgence of power as the Hittites succeed in annihilating the powerful Mitanni kingdom in northern Mesopotamia. In their thrust southward, they came into conflict with the northward aspirations of Egypt. Ramses II stopped the Hittites at Kadesh on the Orontes River (1278 B.C.), but the battle proved so costly that Ramses was constrained to conclude a nonaggression pact with them.

By 1200 B.C., Hittite power in Asia Minor was broken, perhaps by the same movement of peoples that brought the Philistines into Palestine. But centers of Hittite influence[8] remained in Syria for some time at such places as Carchemish and Hamath. When these in turn fell prey to the Assyrian conquerors, the Hittites disappeared from history as an independent power.

As a component of the population of Palestine that Israel did not destroy under Joshua, the Hittites continue to be mentioned in the Biblical record down through the period of the Babylonian exile and after. Ezra complains that "the people of Israel . . . have not separated themselves from . . . the Hittites" (9:1).

Sumer, Ur, and the Mesopotamian Plain

Here, too, thousands of years of profane history become sacred history as God used the nations of this area for His purposes. The review again must be restricted to events that are pertinent to the *Heilsgeschichte* of Scripture and that help to explain its background.

Just as Egypt at the western end of the so-called Fertile Crescent was the Land of the Nile, so the area to the east is dominated by two rivers, the Tigris and the Euphrates.[9] Flowing parallel to each other for some distance, they watered the plain between them

---

[8]Some of these centers played a part in the history of Solomon (1 Kings 10:28–29; 11:1).

[9]The latter is so significant that the Old Testament world can refer to it as simply "the River" (Joshua 24:2–3).

and made possible the construction of a network of irrigation canals. It is not surprising that ancient civilizations flourished in this fertile river valley. But unprotected by such natural barriers as gave Egypt a greater isolation, the Mesopotamian plain saw almost endless turmoil and conflict. Peoples and races from all directions inundated it by infiltration and conquest, achieved control, and then lost it to the next wave of invasion.

Historians customarily call this land of the rivers "Mesopotamia" (the land "in the middle of the rivers"). But this apt designation is of Greek origin and is therefore not found in the Hebrew Old Testament (but cf. Acts 2:9; 7:2). Where the term does occur in our English Bibles, it substitutes for the Hebrew term *Aram-naharaim* (so transliterated by the KJV in the heading of Ps. 60), meaning "Aram [Syria] of the two rivers." Thus, strictly speaking, Mesopotamia in our English Old Testament denotes a general territory in the northern part of this whole area (e.g., the home of Laban, Gen. 24:10; cf. also Deut. 23:4; Judg. 3:8; 1 Chron. 1:26).

"Shinar," another Old Testament term (Gen. 10:10; 14:1; Is. 11:11; Dan. 1:2; Zech. 5:11), often seems to denote particularly the southern part of Mesopotamia.

UR OF THE CHALDEES

Covenant history begins where southern Mesopotamia begins—in the city of Ur. This city was situated near the Persian Gulf in southern Iraq.

When the curtain of written history rises (about 3000 B.C.), Ur and all of southern Mesopotamia were occupied and controlled by a non-Semitic people, the Sumerians. Between 2400 and 2200, Sumerian supremacy was replaced by that of the Semites, who established their headquarters at Akkad at the northern extremity of Sumerian territory. From there the Semites extended their control southward to the Persian Gulf and northward to include all of Mesopotamia. The armed forces of this Akkadian Empire even reached the Mediterranean Sea. These people did not destroy but absorbed much of the Sumerian culture. Thus they adopted the cuneiform (wedge-form) writing of the Sumerians and adapted it to their language. By 2100 the city of Ur came into prominence in a renaissance of Sumerian influence and attained its highest point of commercial and political activity and influence. Known as the Third Dynasty of Ur, its rulers dominated Mesopotamia until about 1950 B.C. After that, the Sumerians lost their identity completely as the result of new disorders and new waves of invaders.

At that point of change (perhaps because of it?) God called Abraham to begin his journey of faith. He was born and reared in an environment and culture far different from that of a nomadic wanderer.

The Old Testament at times refers to Abraham's homeland as "Ur of the Chaldeans," but the Chaldeans were a Semitic people who entered and dominated this territory a whole millennium later. The phrase "of the Chaldeans" probably was added to the text of Gen. 15:7 by a scribe to define the location of Ur for readers of a much later time when Ur had long vanished from memory. The writer of Neh. 9:7 adds this phrase apparently for the same reason, as does Luke in Acts 7:4. This presents no problem for the Bible student, for it is similar to the way people usually refer to Abraham even before Gen. 17:5, when God changed this man's name from "Abram" to "Abraham."

Babylonia

Some 250 miles north of Ur lies Babel (or in its Greek form, Babylon). It is mentioned more often in the Old Testament (256 times) than any other non-Israelite place name.

When the centralized control of the Third Dynasty of Ur broke down, Babylon was able to exploit the inter-Sumerian rivalry to achieve a fame that endured for centuries. Babylonia[10] came to be synonymous with lower Mesopotamia.

The founders of the Old Babylonian Kingdom (1800–1550 B.C.) were Amorites, a branch of the Semitic family that had migrated into the area along the Euphrates. They also settled as far north as Syria and as far west as Transjordania.[11] The sixth king of the Amorite dynasty was the famous Hammurabi (1728–1689 B.C.[12]). By skillful political and military maneuvers, he made Babylon the capital of an empire that extended from the Persian Gulf to the far northern reaches of Mesopotamia. (This first period of Babylonian supremacy had no direct contact with Biblical history.)

Hammurabi's code of 282 laws, inscribed on diorite rock, provides a picture of the social, political, and ethical structure in which much *Heilsgeschichte* transpired. Hammurabi did not create these laws; he merely codified existing practices and earlier

---

[10]"Babylonia" is a Greek formation and does not occur in the Hebrew Old Testament.

[11]For their occupation of Canaan, see Gen. 48:22; Joshua 24:15.

[12]Formerly, Hammurabi was given a much earlier date. Now some scholars date him as late as 1704 to 1662 B.C.

Sumerian customs. Nor was he the first to do so. Codes centuries older have been discovered.

There is no reason, therefore, why a similar "Law Book of Israel" should be called a copy of Hammurabi's and something not indigenous to the Mosaic period some 300 years later. Abraham originally had lived in a society governed by laws similar to Hammurabi's. Nor should it surprise us that some laws in the Pentateuch have close parallels in Hammurabi's code. God did not create a unique new social order for His people but used an existing framework, adapting many of its outward forms for His purposes. Israel's social and economic structure was important not because it was wholly unlike any other but because it was a means to a holy end.

THE NEO-BABYLONIAN EMPIRE

After 1550 B.C. Babylonian glory vanished. Almost a millennium intervenes before God let the power of Babylon become a deciding factor in the history of His people. In the meantime, a Hittite campaign in 1530 destroyed the city of Babylon. In 1500 the Kassites, a non-Semitic people from the northeast, invaded the area and held sway until 1150. Then followed another five centuries of subservience to the Assyrians.

The Neo-Babylonian Empire (625–539 B.C.) began to take shape when the father of Nebuchadnezzar permanently freed Babylon from the Assyrian yoke. The empire is also called the Chaldean Empire because its founders were the Chaldeans, another Semitic people who established themselves along the Persian Gulf.

Nebuchadnezzar ascended the throne in 605 B.C. As a general under his father, he had already subdued all opposition in Mesopotamia and had penetrated victoriously through Syria and Canaan to the borders of Egypt. Returning home through Canaan to assume the throne, he took with him as hostages Daniel and his companions. The Babylonian exile had begun for God's people.

Efforts by Judah's kings to renounce this foreign domination resulted in a siege of Jerusalem in 598 B.C. King Jehoiachin was taken captive along with many of Jerusalem's upper stratum, including the prophet Ezekiel. When Zedekiah, the last king of Judah, revolted, Nebuchadnezzar's patience gave out. He destroyed Jerusalem and the temple in 587/586 and brought a large contingent of captives to Babylon.

Neither he nor his successors inflicted particularly harsh measures on the exiles, who enjoyed considerable freedom and could amass wealth. Some even preferred to remain in the land of their exile when the Babylonian Empire disappeared in 539 B.C. and they were free to return home.

Assyria

Before Nebuchadnezzar made himself master of Canaan in 605 B.C., the kings of Israel and Judah long had been the vassals of the Assyrian Empire, a Semitic people closely related to the Babylonians. Babylon was situated on the lower Euphrates; the Assyrians had their base of operation in Nineveh on the banks of the Tigris in northern Mesopotamia. The land and people derived their name from the old capital city, Asshur (which, in turn, designated their chief deity).

The opportunity for Assyria to develop into an empire came toward the end of the 12th century B.C. The weak Kassite rule in Babylonia was at its end; Hittite power had been broken; Egypt was impotent. By 1100 B.C. Assyrian armies had reached the Mediterranean Sea. But an interval of two centuries of Assyrian weakness followed, during which time David and Solomon arose to establish and expand their kingdom.

Less than a century after Solomon's kingdom had been divided in 932 B.C., the Northern Kingdom (Israel) faced the Assyrian war machine. King Ahab's forces formed part of a coalition of smaller nations that temporarily checked the advance of Shalmaneser III at Qarqar in 853 B.C. Only 11 years later, however, King Jehu became Shalmaneser's tribute-paying vassal. Another century of Assyrian weakness intervened before the Lord would "whistle . . . for the bee that is in the land of Assyria" (Is. 7:18) to sting to death the Northern Kingdom and to force the Southern Kingdom (Judah) into abject submission. Shalmaneser V captured the capital of Israel in 722 B.C., removed 27,290 of its inhabitants, and settled them as captives in other parts of his domain.

The Southern Kingdom saved itself from a similar fate by submitting to Assyrian overlordship. Although the forces of Sennacherib (704–681 B.C.) were halted by God's miraculous intervention in 701, the Assyrian yoke remained on Judah's neck.

When Ashurbanipal (669–633 B.C.) invaded the land of the Nile and destroyed the city of Thebes, Assyria's empire was at its height. But the end was soon to come. Nineveh fell in 612 B.C. A remnant of Assyrian forces made a last stand in northern Syria, but they were defeated six years later. The victors were the Chaldean Babylonians under Nebuchadnezzar, along with the Scythians and the Medes. That year Nebuchadnezzar passed through Jerusalem to take Daniel (as mentioned above).

Persia

Both Assyria and Babylon were Semitic peoples and extended their control over Canaan from bases in Mesopotamia. The next world power was not Semitic but Indo-European; its home territory was not in Mesopotamia but to the east of the Tigris-Euphrates valley (modern Iran). Its ultimate domain included not only the Fertile Crescent and Egypt but stretched from India to Greece. It was the Medo-Persian Empire.

About 1500 B.C. the Medes and the Persians began to flow from Europe into the plateau lands north and east of the Mesopotamian Valley. At first the Medes played a dominant role, especially as they joined with Babylon in the destruction of Assyrian power. In the division of spoils, the Babylonians were allotted most of the western territories formerly held by the Assyrians, while the Medes claimed the areas in the north and east.

Twenty years later the hegemony passed from the Medes to the Persians under Cyrus II (559–530 B.C.), who himself was the son of a Medean princess. He deserves the title of "the Great," for it was not long before he ruled over an empire that extended in a wide swath from his capital east of the Persian Gulf to Asia Minor (Croesus of Lydia). In 539 he took the city of Babylon and added the domains of the Babylonian Empire, including Canaan and Egypt, to his vast holdings. His empire lasted two centuries until it was absorbed by the conquest of Alexander the Great.

The Persian rulers were more tolerant than the previous Semitic emperors. Cyrus permitted the Jewish exiles to return to their homeland. During the reign of his grandson Darius (522–486 B.C.), the rebuilding of the temple in Jerusalem was completed.

The Old Testament closes with the building of the walls of Jerusalem by Nehemiah, cupbearer of Artaxerxes I (465–423 B.C.).

Syria

The top of the Fertile Crescent arch derives its name from a people that occupied various sections of this territory: the Syrians, or more accurately, the Aramaeans.[13]

---

[13]The Latin Bible translated the Hebrew *Aram* incorrectly as Syria, and this term has remained in use since then. Syria, as used in Old Testament history, must not be confused with the Syria of the New Testament, a Roman province, nor with all of modern Syria.

As a geographic term in the Old Testament, Syria denotes the territory north of Canaan to the Taurus Mountains and eastward from Phoenicia and the Mediterranean Sea into the Euphrates Valley.

In lower Mesopotamia, from where Abraham came, Aramaeans (Syrians) are known as early as 1900 B.C. The area where Abraham next settled (after leaving Ur and before his migration to Canaan) and where his brother Nahor's descendants, Bethuel and Laban, remained is called *Padan Aram* ("field/road of Syria") in Gen. 25:20. In this verse both Bethuel and Laban are called Syrians.

Racially, the Syrians were closely related to the Israelites, who were instructed to say, "My father was a Syrian" (i.e., Abraham and Jacob; Deut. 26:5). Amos reminds his hearers that they were the chosen people only by divine grace, and that they were only one among many nations whose destinies God directed. He includes the Syrians as one of the examples. "Did I not bring up Israel from the land of Egypt, the Philistines from Caphtor, and the Syrians from Kir?" (Amos 9:7; cf. 2 Kings 16:9; Is. 22:6).[14]

By 1300 B.C. large settlements of Syrians (Aramaeans) existed in the area west of the Euphrates, the area the Bible calls Syria. The various small and independent kingdoms that developed there are differentiated in the Old Testament (e.g., the Syria of Zoba[h], of Beth Rehob, of Ish-Tob, of Maacah, of Geshur, of Damascus; 2 Sam 8:3–6; 10:6; 15:8).

David extended his rule into Syria as far north as Hamath (2 Sam. 8:9–12). During and after Solomon's reign, a strong and independent Syrian kingdom came into existence under the leadership of the city of Damascus. Whenever Assyrian pressure from the east was relaxed, this Syrian confederacy sought to expand southward at the expense of the Northern Kingdom (Israel). Thus Ben-Hadad of Damascus, with the aid of 32 kings, besieged Samaria at the time of Ahab (1 Kings 20:1–25). This attempt to take Samaria, as well as the campaign when he "mustered the Syrians" the following spring, failed (1 Kings 20:26–34). Later Syrian invasions were successful, and for a time northern Israel was reduced almost to a state of vassalage (2 Kings 10:32–33; 13:1–7). The Syrians even captured the southern city of Gath in the Philistine plains and threatened Jerusalem (2 Kings 12:17–18).

Assyrian advances westward into Syria enabled Israel to regain its lost territory. When shortly thereafter a period of Assyrian

---

[14]The location of Kir has not been established.

decline set in, Jeroboam II of Israel (783–743 B.C.) invaded the weakened Syria and "recaptured for Israel, from Damascus and Hamath, what had belonged to Judah" (2 Kings 14:28). Syria never regained its strength or glory. Tiglath-Pileser of Assyria annexed Syria and in 732 B.C. destroyed the city of Damascus.

Though Syria did not find fame by force of arms, Aramaic, the language of this strategically situated land, achieved international and lasting influence. By the time of the Babylonian captivity, Aramaic even had replaced spoken Hebrew[15] and would become the popular language at the time of Jesus.

Other Peoples Within Canaan

Several peoples were associated with covenant history from the beginning. Abraham did not find Canaan an open and unpopulated land, but "the Canaanites were then in the land" (Gen. 12:6). Some of these early inhabitants have been mentioned—for example, the Hittites and the Philistines. In promising to give Abraham's descendants the land wherein he was a stranger, God specified no less than 10 peoples from whom He would take the land (Gen. 15:18–21). The names of two of these nations are at times also used comprehensively to designate the entire population of the land: the Canaanites and the Amorites.

THE CANAANITES

The term *Canaan* appears to have been derived originally from a common noun denoting purple wool.[16] It was then applied to the land in which the wool was produced. And a "canaanite" was a trader or merchant of purple.[17]

Some passages in the Old Testament reflect this original use of the word *canaanite* as a common noun (Ezek. 16:29; 17:4; Zeph. 1:11), where it is properly translated as "merchant" or "trader." Perhaps this term originally was restricted to Phoenicia, for Isaiah (23:8) says that the princes of Tyre were "canaanites," that is, merchants. The term was then applied to wider areas, even the entire land of Canaan and all its inhabitants (as, for example, in Gen. 12:6, quoted above).

Besides this general use, "Canaanite" also appears to identify

---

[15]Parts of Ezra and Daniel and one verse in Jeremiah are written in Aramaic.

[16]The dye was extracted from a Mediterranean shellfish by the Phoenicians (in Greek: the "people of purple").

[17]For a similar word connection, cf. "calico" and "Calcutta."

a part of the population as distinct from other strains, such as the Hittites, the Perizzites, the Hivites, and the Jebusites (Ex. 3:8, 17). These Canaanites are found on both sides of the Jordan (Joshua 11:3) and seem to be almost everywhere (Judg. 1:9–10). No doubt the people, when distinguished as such, are closely related to the people and culture of Phoenicia, the territory where the name originated. But in some instances the Old Testament reader (as well as the translator) finds it hard to determine whether "Canaanite" is used in a general or restricted sense and what the basis for the differentiation is.

THE AMORITES

The term *Amorites* also is used sometimes in a general way of the entire population, though not as often as *Canaanite*. Amos reminds his people that God gave them the Promised Land when He "destroyed the Amorite before them" (Amos 2:9; cf. Gen. 15:16; Deut. 1:27). In Joshua 10:5–6, "all the kings of the Amorites" include people of various tribal affinities.

But "Amorite" is also used to distinguish these people from others (Num. 13:29), particularly from the Canaanites.[18] The spies whom Moses had sent into Canaan from the desert reported that the Amalekites dwell in the land of Negev; the Hittites, the Jebusites, and the Amorites in the hill country; and the Canaanites by the sea and along the Jordan (Num. 13:29).

When Israel came out of the desert, the territory east of the Jordan and north of the Arnon River was in the possession of two Amorite kings, Sihon and Og (Num. 21:13, 21–26, 33–35). As already indicated, Israel found them also on the western side of the Jordan among the Canaanites, whose language and culture were similar to theirs. Remnants of the Amorites still existed and were identified as such at the time of David and Solomon (2 Sam. 21:2; 1 Kings 9:20).

THE HIVITES (HORITES)

According to Ex. 3:17, Moses is to tell the Israelites that God will bring them "to the land of the Canaanites and the Hittites and the Amorites and the Perizzites and the Hivites and the Jebusites." At the time of the conquest, the Hivites are mentioned as occupying various parts of the land (Joshua 9:7, 17—in Gibeon,

---

[18]In Deut. 3:9 the Sidonian (Phoenician) name of a city is distinguished from its Amorite name.

etc.; 11:3—below Hermon; Judg. 3:3—in Lebanon). They appear as an identifiable group as late as David's time (2 Sam. 24:7).

The origin and ethnic affiliation of the Hivites have not been established. Because they were uncircumcised (Gen. 34), it has been suggested that they were non-Semitic. The Hivites might well be identified with the Horites. In Genesis 34:2 and Joshua 9:7 the early Greek translation of the Old Testament (the Septuagint) actually reads "Horites" for "Hivites"—only a slight change in the original. If in these instances as well as in others the Greek text is to be preferred, then a great deal about the "Hivites" is known.

The Hurrians, as they are called in extra-Biblical sources, played an important role in Near Eastern history. They entered Mesopotamia from the north about 2000 B.C. in so large and persistent a stream that they were able to form strong kingdoms in the entire area from the Euphrates to beyond the Tigris. One of these, the kingdom of the Mitanni (about 1500 to 1360 B.C.), was strong enough to represent the balance of power in the days of the Egyptian and Hittite expansion. Haran, the city from which Abraham left for Canaan, was located within their sphere of influence. The Hurrian city of Nuzi, east of the Tigris, has since 1925 yielded several thousand tablets. From them it appears that the customs and laws that prevailed there were similar to those reflected in the patriarchal stories.

If "Hivites" should read as "Horites" in the Old Testament, this strain of the Canaanite population must have been the result of migrations by these invaders into Syria and the Promised Land.[19]

THE REPHAIM AND OTHERS

Rephaim are mentioned as living on both sides of the Jordan and are known in various areas by different names, such as Emim, Anakim, and Zanzumim. Perhaps Rephaim is a term to denote people of tall stature and is used in connection with groups of various ethnic derivations.

Other less important people are the Kennites, the Kenezzites, the Kadmonites, the Perizzites, and the Girgashites (Gen. 15:19–21).

---

[19]The earlier inhabitants of Edom are also called Horites (Gen. 14:6; 36:20–21; Deut. 2:12, 22), but it is questionable whether they can be linked with the Hurrians.

The Peoples Adjacent to Palestine[20]

THE EDOMITES

The Edomites, south of the Dead Sea, were close kin to Israel. Their ancestor, Esau, was Jacob's twin brother (Gen. 25), and the twins' rivalry lived on in their descendants into New Testament history. Already on their journey from Egypt to take possession of Canaan, the Israelites were refused passage through the mountainous territory of Edom (Num. 20:14–21). And Amos later wrote, "[Edom] pursued his brother with the sword, and cast off all pity; his anger tore perpetually, and he kept his wrath forever" (1:11; cf. Is. 34:5–17; Ezek. 35 [esp. v. 15]; Obad.). As a result, Edom became the symbol and representative of all anti-God forces (as did Babylon in the New Testament) that obstruct the course of His kingdom. (Cf. Amos 9:11–12; Is. 63.)

Saul and David campaigned successfully against them (1 Sam. 14:47; 2 Sam. 8:13–15). After Solomon's time, Edom regained its independence, and domination by Judah was only sporadic. When Nebuchadnezzar destroyed Jerusalem in 587/586 B.C., the Edomites moved northward into the depopulated territory of Judah (Ezek. 35:10; 36:5). In the New Testament the Edomites are called Idumaeans, and their rivalry with Israel can still be seen in the appointment of the Idumaean-related Herods over the Israelites.

THE MOABITES

To the north of Edom, along the east side of the Dead Sea up to the Arnon River, the Moabites established their homeland. They were related to the Israelites by their descent from Lot, Abraham's nephew (Gen. 19:37). The Moabites also refused the Israelites passage through their territory and forced Moses to skirt it on the east (Num. 21:10–13). After the occupation of Canaan by Joshua, the Moabites continued to play a role in the history of Israel. Prophets from Amos to Ezekiel include them in their oracles of doom on foreign nations. And Ezra (9:1) and Nehemiah (13:23) mention them as a source of temptation for the people of the covenant in postexilic times.

---

[20]The territory of the five peoples discussed here (Edom, Moab, Ammon, Midian, and Amalek) constitute the eastern and southern extent of David's empire.

THE AMMONITES

The Ammonites, also descendants of Lot (Gen. 19:38), settled north of the Moabites between the Amorite kingdom along the Jordan and the desert on the east. Israelite contact with the Ammonites began at the time of the judges and continued into post-exilic times.

THE MIDIANITES

The Midianites, a nomadic people descended from Abraham and Ketura (Gen. 25:4), appear at various places in and outside of Canaan and in association with a number of other groups. In the Joseph account (Gen. 37:25–27), they are mentioned with the Ishmaelites.[21] Later, after Moses had fled from Egypt, he married a daughter of a local Midianite priest, Jethro (Raguel), and kept his flock for 40 years (Ex. 2:15–22). In spite of that, the Midianites in Moab made common cause against Israel. At the time of the judges, the Midianites were in league with the Amalekites and "the people of the East" in their raid into Israel (Judg. 6:3).

No doubt the Midianites were a loose aggregation of nomadic tribes whose center was along the Gulf of Aqaba and east of Edom. From there they radiated in pursuit of various enterprises. Related to them are the Kenites, descendants of Moses' Midianite father-in-law. They separated themselves from their fellow tribesmen before King Saul defeated the Amalekites "from Havilah all the way to Shur, which is east of Egypt" (1 Sam. 15:1–7). The Midianites did not thereafter threaten Israel, nor are they among the peoples on whom the prophets pronounced doom.

THE AMALEKITES

On the western side of the Gulf of Aqaba, between Sinai and southwestern Palestine, lived other descendants of Esau: the Amalekites (Gen. 36:2–4, 12). They were the first to harass the Israelites shortly after they had escaped from Egypt. At Rephidim, while Moses prayed with uplifted arms, the Amalekites were defeated by Joshua (Ex. 17:8–13). In the period of the judges, the Amalekites made inroads into Canaan in alliance with the Moabites and the Ammonites (Judg. 3:13) and the Midianites (Judg. 6:3; 7:12). Saul defeated the Amalekites, and after David's time they disappear as a people (1 Sam. 27:8–9; 30:1–20).

---

[21]Ishmael was the son of Abraham and Hagar (Gen. 16).

3. Genesis

Genesis recounts events prior to the formation of Israel as God's covenant nation. The succeeding books in the Old Testament record what God did for and through Israel. Therefore, Genesis is often said to present a prehistory to the main content of the Old Testament. But it is more than that.

Genesis should also be viewed in the larger perspective of the entire "mystery of revelation" leading through Israel to God's final act of salvation in Jesus Christ. When Paul, for example (in Gal. 3:16–25), reviews the entire Old Testament period "till the Seed [Christ] should come" (v. 19), the covenant with Abraham is not preliminary but basic to God's entire plan of salvation. All that followed, including the covenant at Sinai, implemented the promise to Abraham. At Mount Sinai the law "was added because of transgressions" (v. 19), as a "tutor" (v. 24) to remind humanity constantly of its sinfulness and need for redemption.

The entire history of Israel, therefore, may actually be considered a grand interlude between the promise to Abraham and its fulfillment in Jesus Christ. The Sinai covenant of Law did not annul the promise but represents the way God chose "that the promise by faith in Jesus Christ might be given to those who believe" (v. 22). Israel was elected to inherit and bear the promise of grace; the covenant of Mount Sinai was to remind Israel constantly of its need for grace and at the same time to assure it that God's plan of salvation was being carried out. True, the covenant of Sinai had provisional aspects, but they were only a means to an end. Since they now have served their purpose, "we are no longer under a tutor" (v. 25). The covenant with Abraham, therefore, was not merely first but also preeminent and permanent. Its promise underlies all God's deeds for and through Israel. In the framework of such a *Heilsgeschichte*, all the accounts of Genesis have meaning and relevance.

Genesis has also been rightly called "the book of beginnings," for it recounts how the world and humanity began, how marriage originated, how people became sinful, how God directed the affairs of nations during the first millennia of history. But beneath this compressed recital of events from Adam to Abraham's grandsons lies the principle that controlled the selection and presentation of the materials themselves—God's desire to portray Himself as fulfilling His promise to bring salvation. God, who promised to redeem humanity, created the universe and therefore has the power to direct all things to achieve His purpose. The sin of the first parents—and of their offspring, begotten in their marred image of God—establishes the need for the saving acts of God's grace. In a selective and schematic account of the nations, general world history quickly narrows to Abraham, the father of believers.

The events in Genesis introduce the book of Exodus, but they also provide the proper perspective for the entire Old Testament as well as the New. Genesis emphasizes that salvation is by the promise of grace and not through the Law—and that the succeeding history of Israel recounts God in action to fulfill that promise. As such, Genesis controls the interpretation of the entire Old Testament by writing across each page: Abraham *"believed God and it was accounted to him for righteousness"* (Gal. 3:6; cf. Gen. 15:6).

The call of Abraham, therefore, divides Genesis into two majestic pillars that bear up the temple of Scripture—not only the vestibule but its entire sublime edifice. If we pull them down, we have not removed a supposedly inconsequential foreword to the Bible but foundational truths that support the whole structure of Biblical teaching. These two pillars of truth are

1. The God of the covenant is the eternal and almighty Creator, and His foremost yet rebellious creature needs redeeming mercy (Gen. 1–11).
2. The God of the universe, a gracious Creator, initiated covenant history in order to restore fallen humanity (Gen. 12–50).[1]

1. Genesis 1 to 11

THE CREATOR

The first verse of Genesis already contains one of its most sublime and profound lessons. Seven clipped Hebrew words usher us into the presence of the sovereign Creator of the universe. Knowing Him to be the God of the covenant, we are immediately assured that He does not lack the power to execute His plan of salvation. And the verse makes equally clear that our relationship to God does not depend on what we think or do but on His deeds.

Human thought, in its attempt to comprehend this God who existed before "the beginning," reaches an impassable barrier. Humans live in time and space but do not understand how these

---

[1]The following sections on chaps. 1–11 and 12–50 mention briefly only some of the basic teachings of Genesis that underlie the Christian religion and make it unique.

dimensions came to be or how and why they determine their being. Yet, says Genesis, God existed before time and space appear "in the beginning."

> Before the mountains were brought forth, or ever You had formed the earth and the world, even from everlasting to everlasting, You are God. . . . For a thousand years in Your sight are like yesterday when it is past, and like a watch in the night" (Ps. 90:2, 4).

The name of God occurs 34 times in the first 35 verses (Gen. 1:1–2:4) to underscore the absolute cleavage between who He is and what He causes to be.

THE CREATION PROCESS

By the distinction between Creator and creature, between the eternal, absolute God and what began "in the beginning," Genesis rejects all false cosmogonies and theogonies (theories of the origin of the universe and of God) ancient and modern, all the myths of pantheism and materialism, of polytheism and atheism. Heaven and earth—that is, the universe—are not an emanation of a divine substance; God created them. He "calls into existence the things that do not exist" (Rom. 4:17 RSV). "He spoke, and it was done; He commanded, and it stood fast" (Ps. 33:9). And both the Creator and what He created[2] were "good" (Gen. 1:31)—that is, without sin. No destructive or disruptive forces vitiated the harmony and purpose of the works of His hands.

This world-view determines everything that follows in the Bible. Genesis 1 is not a humanly demonstrable and verifiable item of history; no human was there to report what occurred. It is an article of faith, "the evidence of things not seen" (Heb. 11:1). Human reason may deduce the existence of a creator, but to accept all the implications of Gen. 1:1 requires another creative work, that of the *Creator Spiritus.*

Only the "new man," who by the Spirit of God says that Jesus is Lord (1 Cor. 12:3), understands by faith "that the worlds were framed by the word of God, so that the things which are seen were not made of things which are visible" (Heb. 11:3). Only the believer, chosen "before the foundation of the world" (Eph. 1:4) in Christ, who "was in the beginning with God" (John 1:2), can

---

[2]Scripture uses the Hebrew word for *create* exclusively with God as the subject. The Bible also uses such words as "fashion," "form," and "make" of God, but the limits of the analogy between human activity and God's creating are explicitly set forth and safeguarded.

praise the Lord, who laid that foundation of the earth. And only the believer awaits the "evidence of things not seen"—the creation of the new heaven and the new earth (Rev. 21:1).

Though this world-view requires faith, it brooks no other view. Every explanation of the origin of the universe that does not say, "In the beginning God created the heaven and the earth," results in worship of idols of human creation and/or deifies forces of nature.

This idolatry is crassly evident in ancient creation myths. For example, the Babylonian epic *Enuma Elish* antedates the Genesis account but has a vastly different literary form and structure. Its surface similarities in content are slight in comparison with the wide gulf that separates its basic concepts from those of the first page of the Bible. These differences can be briefly summarized as follows:

1. *Enuma Elish* is grossly polytheistic.
2. The firmament and the earth are the remains of a slain goddess rather than the result of a fiat creation by God's Word.
3. There is, therefore, no creation "in the beginning" but merely a reshaping of animated material that is itself uncreated.
4. Evil and good (dualism) existed in the gods before the beginning, and the creation of the world is but one result of the struggle between these principles.

Genesis, therefore, is not merely another account or a slight improvement on the Babylonian story; the two are antithetical world-views.

Modern myths also stand condemned before Genesis 1—and for the same reason. Except for terminology, they contain nothing new.

1. Like the many gods of Babylonia, uncreated forces of nature bring about the universe.
2. Like the struggle between the gods, some process cleaves and assembles matter.
3. Instead of a Creator who is above, beyond, and different from the creature, the universe has in itself what makes it come into being.

Every science that is not predicated on and does not operate with a Creator of heaven and earth dethrones the God of the Bible and makes humanity a piece of flotsam bobbing aimlessly on a sea of polytheistic/pantheistic/materialistic powers. Evolution is ultimately pure ignorance; for it says, "Everything was created by no one out of nothing."

HUMANITY

Genesis lists Adam and Eve as the last of God's creatures not because they are an afterthought but because they excel all of them and climax God's creation story.

The account is sublime in its simplicity and brevity. But its anthropology (teaching regarding humans) posits another foundation stone on which the whole Bible depends for its meaning and message: Humanity is not divine.

In the Babylonian creation epic, heaven and earth spring from the cleft corpse of a goddess. Humanity springs from the blood of her evil consort.

But according to Genesis 1, humanity is distinct from God just as are the animals; all become "living creatures" of the immutable and sovereign Creator, who transcends what He has made.

Yet men and women are godlike in a way that no animal is; they were created "in the image of God" (Gen. 1:27). Though the image was not a physical likeness (for God is a spirit), when God "breathed into his nostrils the breath of life; and man became a living being" (2:7), Adam and Eve were given a share in the "dominion over" all created things (1:28). They also possessed spiritual, psychical, voluntative, and rational powers so that they could understand and respond to God when He said, "you may" and "you shall not" (2:16–17). This part of Adam and Eve was also "very good." Body and soul, in a psychosomatic unity, functioned in the perfect relationship and communion with the Creator for which He had designed human beings.

This explanation of human origin cannot be harmonized with a theory of transformation from lower to higher forms of life. The image of God did not spring from subhuman flesh and blood or from natural forces or material. Evolution, without the creative, sovereign, and transcendent God, flatly contradicts the distinction between human and animal on which rests not only Genesis but the entire Bible.

HUMANITY, THE FALLEN CREATURE

Genesis 1, in its comprehensive presentation of the origin of the entire universe, includes the creation of human beings. This sets the stage for the history of humanity, which begins in Gen. 2:4. The remaining verses of chapter 2 elaborate on the creation of humanity as male and female (1:27) and delineate the relationship of the created earth and animals to human beings, who have "dominion . . . over all the earth" (1:26).

But above all, humanity's relationship to the Creator is clearly set forth in chapter 2. Adam's communion with the life-giving God will continue unless he oversteps the bounds of his creatureliness by disobedience to God and aspires to be equal with God.

Chapter 3 tells the sad story of the first couple's rebellion against their Creator. It is not an abstract treatise on the origin of evil per se. Rather, it tells us that Adam and Eve *did* evil and so became subject to death. The eating of the forbidden fruit was the declaration and the signal of their rebellion against the limitations of their creatureliness. It was their attempt to be like the omniscient God, "knowing good and evil." This baleful act the Bible later calls "sin." It disrupted Adam's and Eve's blissful relationship with God, with each other, with the animals, and with nature itself. This total corruption and estrangement, an uncontrollable disposition to defy God and His will, we call original sin, because every offspring of Adam is like Seth, the son of Adam, begotten "in his [Adam's] own likeness, after his image" (Gen. 5:3).

Genesis 3 shows the need for all subsequent chapters and books of the Bible, where (as already in Gen. 3:15) God promises to deliver us from sin and death and records what He did to remove these barriers that exclude us from life with Him. The message of all Scripture is that God Himself, in the Seed of the woman, will crush the head of "that serpent of old, called the Devil and Satan, who deceives the whole world" (Rev. 12:9).

SIN

Immediately after the Fall, chapters 4–11 reveal the corroding power of sin in human beings: Already the first generation of natural-born humans commits murder (Cain; chap. 4). Ultimately, "the wickedness of man was [so] great in the earth" (6:5) that God sent the deluge to destroy all but eight souls (chaps. 6–8).

Sin itself did not drown in the flood but lived on in Noah and his descendants (11:10–32). In 11:1–9 we see it uniting people in an organized rebellion against the Creator and their dependence on Him: the Tower of Babel. But solidarity and cooperation in sin, far from dethroning God, resulted in the curse of division, for "the LORD confused the language of all the earth" (Gen. 11:9).

THE MERCY OF GOD IN SPITE OF SIN

These first chapters of Genesis portray the dark onslaught of sin and its wages of death. But they also reveal that the rays of God's mercy toward the sinner break through this gloom. They tell that God at once graciously promised deliverance from the effects and power of sin—the promise given to Adam and Eve. The genealogies of their descendants to Abraham (Gen. 11) trace the lineage from which the woman's Seed is to come. These dry lists of names are the first *Heilsgeschichte* in barest outline. As God made clear in the case of Noah, even in the world of perverse humanity He will carry forward His plan of salvation from generation to generation.

FACT OR FICTION?

On these great truths of Gen. 1–11 rests the whole structure of the Bible. They are not myths—that is, fanciful explanations that have no basis in actual fact or event—but God's own description of the facts. Furthermore, these truths are taught in a perfect form of communication that never needs revision. People of all ages can understand and believe that the world owes its origin to the creative acts of God.

The language of the creation account has been called "phenomenal," meaning that it describes the phenomena of the world as it would and does appear to human observation. Thus, the scientist who explores the wonders of creation's microcosms and macrocosms has no reason to revise the opening hymn of Genesis: "In the beginning God created the heavens and the earth."

But there has been a difference of opinion among Christian interpreters as to what extent Genesis teaches the "how" of creation—beyond the fact that it was accomplished as the result of God's command, "Let there be. . . ." The ancient creeds and the Lutheran Confessions simply say, "I believe in God, . . . Maker of heaven and earth."

Some believe that the creation account leaves the process wrapped in the mystery of anthropomorphic and figurative language. After all, when Scripture reports that "God said," no one should believe in a crassly literal view of God with human vocal chords that produce audible sounds. Similarly, they hold, when "the day [singular] that the LORD God made the earth and the heavens" (2:4) is divided into six days plus a seventh indeterminate day on which God rested, Scripture is saying figuratively that God's creation resulted in an ordered universe of similarities and distinctions, yet constituting a harmonious whole. Many Christian scientists of today, extending the above, believe that the figurative language of Genesis permits the interpolation of long ages of a creative process between God's creation "in the beginning" and the universe in its present form. On the other hand, the old church father Augustine, in a prescientific age, held the view that

God's act of creation was instantaneous.

Whatever people believe, all of Scripture makes this clear: it is impossible to reduce the language of Genesis to an empty figure of speech and its anthropomorphisms to meaningless myths. It is literally true that the first 11 chapters of Genesis sustain the whole structure of Biblical teaching: *The God of the covenant is the eternal and almighty Creator of the universe and of humanity.*

2. Genesis 12 to 50

The content of Gen. 12–50 also is basic to Scripture and can be likened to another pillar at its entrance. Like the first, it is not a decorative piece of architecture or a facade but a functional and basic support of the structure. Therefore, it can be inscribed: *The God of the universe, a gracious Creator, initiated covenant history to restore fallen humanity.*

The covenant is as much a creation of God as the universe. He created the world by His word of command; He created the covenant by His word of promise. The "everlasting God, the LORD, the Creator of the ends of the earth" (Is. 40:28), He who "made the earth and created man on it" (Is. 45:12), makes clear in the covenant with the patriarchs that not even human events will be "without form, and void" (Gen. 1:2). He will fashion His light to dispel sin's darkness and to bring forth the order of salvation, replacing the chaos of death. In obedience to His "let there be," a chain of situations and circumstances will arise that will fulfill His gracious purpose and enable ungodly people to be renewed "according to the image of Him who created" them (Col. 3:10).

The covenant is more than an example of God's power; it is also the revelation of His divine love and mercy—as unending and unfathomable as His omnipotence. After the Fall, humanity could only offend God, could only compound its guilt and seal its own death. But in the covenant with the patriarchs, God gives the assurance that He is setting in motion a plan of salvation that is entirely the gift of His love. God chooses Abraham, Isaac, and Jacob as the channels of His grace to all people.

The patriarchs themselves demonstrate the inability of human beings to make themselves acceptable to God. As bearers of the promise, they also need the forgiving mercy of God, for without such grace they would be lost and would deserve nothing but wrath and punishment. For this reason, the sacred record paints them not as saints but as sinners both before and after God rescued them. As Joshua reminded the Israelites, "Your fathers, including Terah, the father of Abraham and the father of Nahor, dwelt on the other side of the River [the Euphrates] in old times; and they served other gods" (Joshua 24:2). In his commentary on Genesis, Luther says: "If you should ask what Abraham was before he was called by a merciful God, Joshua 24:2 answers [this question] that he was an idolater, that is, that he deserved death and eternal damnation."[3]

Even after God's love sought them out, ungodliness is evident in their lives. Abraham presumed to correct God's method of giving him the promised offspring; he and Isaac surrendered their wives to assure their own security; Jacob stooped to deceiving his father to obtain the blessing.

The covenant with the patriarchs is, first of all, God's way of making clear the basic and unchanging Scriptural teaching that all people, even the patriarchs, are rescued from death to life because He is the God "who justifies the ungodly" (Rom. 4:5). Salvation from sin and from its resulting separation from God is wholly God's doing. All those—and only those—who enter His covenant and trust its promises of grace receive the unmerited gift of salvation.

The patriarchs also demonstrate how people enter this state of grace. In Gen. 15:6, the word *believe* occurs for the first time in the Bible: "He [Abraham] believed in the LORD" (cf. Rom. 4:3; Gal. 3:6; James 2:23). Abraham is called "the father of all those who believe" (Rom. 4:11) because from him we can learn what faith is and what it does.

When Abraham believed the Lord, his "faith was accounted to [him] for righteousness" (Rom. 4:9). By believing that God would bless and not destroy him as he had deserved, he accepted the forgiving grace of God. No matter what he was or how much "sin abounded" in him, he would be counted right with God if he took refuge in the grace that "abounded much more" (Rom. 5:20). Abraham did not create this covenant and its state of grace; he believed it.

Abraham believed, but he did not live to see the fulfillment of God's great promises; for "faith is the substance of things hoped for, the evidence of things not seen" (Heb. 11:1). God had promised, "All the land which you see I give to you" (Gen. 13:15), but it remained merely the "Land of Promise." All Abraham ever owned in Canaan was a burial plot that was not given to him but was purchased by him. God also promised, "I will make you a great

---

[3]*Lectures on Genesis, Chapters 6–14*, trans. George V. Schick; ed. Jaroslav Pelikan, Daniel E. Poellot, in *Luther's Works*, American Edition, vol. 2 (St. Louis: Concordia Publishing House, 1960): 246.

nation" (12:2), but Abraham remained without an heir until he was "as good as dead" (Heb. 11:12), and it was humanly impossible that one should be born to him. The third part of God's promise said, "In you all the families of the earth shall be blessed" (Gen. 12:3), but Abraham "died in faith, not having received the promises, but having seen them afar off" (Heb. 11:13).

Abraham had no proof of God's promises, only trust in them and in God to carry them out. He did not demand to know the how and when of coming blessings. His faith simply clung to God's promise that they would come in God's good pleasure and time. Therefore, all that God promised to do belonged to Abraham by faith, and Jesus could say to those who with seeing eyes did not see, "Abraham rejoiced to see My day, and he saw it and was glad" (John 8:56).

The father of the believers also gave evidence of the *obedience of faith*. Though his faith at times wavered and gave way to disobedience, he also demonstrated the true nature of faith: to respond to God's grace by submitting to and doing His will. Like faith, obedience requires a total commitment. "By faith Abraham obeyed when he was called to go out. . . . And he went out, not knowing where he was going" (Heb. 11:8). "By faith . . . Abraham offered up his only begotten son . . . concluding that God was able to raise him up, even from the dead" (Heb. 11:17–19).

Abraham's obedience was of faith because, like his faith, it did not create the covenant of grace. For example, Abraham "circumcised his son Isaac when he was eight days old, as God had commanded him" (Gen. 21:4; cf. 17:9–14). Circumcision was the "sign of the covenant" (17:11) because by obeying this command Abraham signified that he was accepting the undeserved blessing that God had promised him in the covenant.

Abraham's obedience was the result of his faith, and therefore he also received the reward of grace: "Do not be afraid, Abram. I am your shield, your exceedingly great reward" (Gen. 15:1). Thus God blessed all Abraham's deeds of faith with the gift of grace that faith itself receives.

The Unfolding of God's Plan of Salvation

God did not first begin to be merciful to His rebellious creatures at the time of the patriarchs. Already with Adam and Eve "in His forbearance God had passed over the sins that were previously committed" (Rom. 3:25) because the sting of death and the power of sin would be absorbed and nullified by the woman's Seed. By virtue of God's forgiving mercy all could again walk with God as "Enoch walked with God; and he was not, for God took him" (Gen. 5:24; cf. Heb. 11:5).

Yet in the covenant with Abraham, Isaac, and Jacob, God reveals more clearly what steps He is taking to accomplish His saving purpose. He is creating a historical process to fulfill His plan in "the fullness of the times [that] He might gather together in one all things in Christ, both which are in heaven and which are on earth" (Eph. 1:10). He selected Abraham and his descendants from all the families of the earth (cf. the genealogies of Gen. 5, 10, 11) that salvation might be "of the Jews" (John 4:22) and "that the blessing of Abraham might come upon the Gentiles in Christ Jesus" (Gal. 3:14).

The accounts of the patriarchs are not complete biographies. Only certain episodes from their lives are recorded,[4] but each one makes its contribution to the overall theme: The God of the covenant is carrying out His promises, but He does it His way. He has His own sovereign reasons for waiting long ages before the old covenant is validated and fulfilled in the blood of the new covenant. And He has His own reason why it is that of "the patriarchs, and of their race, according to the flesh, is the Christ" (Rom. 9:5 RSV). But just as unfathomable was His long-suffering and patience with those whom He had chosen to be the bearers of His promise.

Structure and Outline in Genesis

In summarizing the teachings of Genesis, its contents have been likened to two pillars undergirding all Biblical revelation. The book divides itself into 10 sections, each introduced by the same heading. Arranged in sequence, they constitute a clearly defined outline of the contents of the book. In the KJV these 10 structural units are labeled as follows:

1. The generations of the heavens and the earth: 2:4–4:26
2. The generation of Adam: 5:1–6:8
3. The generation of Noah: 6:9–9:28
4. The generation of the sons of Noah: 10:1–11:9
5. The generation of Shem: 11:10–26
6. The generation of Terah (Abraham's father): 11:27–25:11
7. The generation of Ishmael: 25:12–18
8. The generation of Isaac, Abraham's son: 25:19–35:29
9. The generation of Esau: 36:1–37:1
10. The generation of Jacob: 37:2–50:26

---

[4]Abraham: Gen. 12:1–25:11; Isaac and his sons: 25:12–36:32; Jacob and his sons: 37:1–50:26.

The English word *generations*, which in modern usage suggests timespans, does not adequately convey the meaning of the Hebrew. Nor do other single English words suffice as its equivalent—terms such as "descendants" (RSV), "account" (NIV), "history" or "genealogy" (NKJV). The Hebrew noun *toledoth* derives from the verb meaning "to beget, to procreate, or to produce (a thing)." Therefore, in these headings *toledoth* denotes a series of sequels to events begotten or produced by antecedent circumstances and identified by the name attached to them.

This meaning of the caption is especially important to its use in Gen. 2:4, where it occurs for the first time. For example, it would be misleading to first read, "This is the history of the heavens and the earth," and then to regard what follows as an alternate version of the creation account of 1:1–23. Rather, 2:4 introduces what happened after God had created the universe. Into a setting that was "very good" came the disruptive and diabolical power of sin, committed by a man and a woman who were created in God's image and in harmony with their Creator. The heading in 2:4 introduces a new topic: the fall of humanity and its need of redemption. At the same time, it calls attention to the circumstances in which this tragedy occurred: a perfect world called into existence when "the LORD God made the earth and the heavens."

The remaining nine sections of the outline, introduced by the same formula, likewise are to be understood as sequels "begotten" in a previous era.

• • • • •

What Adam did and came to be is not merely a memory but a sad reality in all people from Adam and Eve through Abraham, Isaac, and Jacob down to today: "Through one man sin entered the world, and death through sin" (Rom. 5:12). There is no exception to the rule: Where there is life, there is death. But another Adam was to come and bring the good news: Where there is death, there is life. "The son of Adam, the son of God" (Luke 3:38), "the last Adam" (1 Cor. 15:45), was and remained "the image of the invisible God" (Col. 1:15). Therefore, "those who receive abundance of grace and of the gift of righteousness will reign in life through the One, Jesus Christ" (Rom. 5:17); for "by Man [*the* Man: Christ] also came the resurrection of the dead" (1 Cor. 15:21).

46

4. Exodus

"I have remembered My covenant" (Ex. 6:5; cf. Ps. 105:8–45).

This word of God to Moses provides the perspective of the place of Exodus in God's unfolding schema of revelation. Its chapters constitute a link with the past and provide the basis for what is to follow throughout covenant history.

To the descendants of Abraham, Isaac, and Jacob, God seemed to have forgotten His covenant; the time seemed endless. "The sojourn of the children of Israel who lived in Egypt was four hundred and thirty years" (Ex. 12:40). During these centuries God apparently had not moved to fulfill His promise to give possession of Canaan to Abraham's descendants. True, the patriarchs had lived temporarily in the Land of Promise, but now the sons of Jacob were again in a foreign land.

Exodus gives no reason for this gap in salvation history, for God alone knows the "times or seasons which the Father has put in His own authority" (Acts 1:7). But these silent years speak loudly of the need to depend on the promises of God, for with Him even a thousand years are but a day (Ps. 90:4), and without Him nothing will or can happen.

"I have remembered My covenant." This statement bridges the intervening time and affirms the patriarchal covenant of grace. What God will do now remains as much a gift of undeserved goodness as the promises given to Abraham. His descendants also will be right with God if they accept the assurance of His forgiving mercy. They, like Abraham, need only to respond to His covenanted gift with an obedience of faith that is unquestioning and unrestrained under the totality of God's claim on them.

Exodus also supplies the basis for subsequent Old Testament books and for understanding the history that is to follow—not merely Israel's history but the covenant history that leads through Abraham's seed in which "all the nations shall be blessed" (Gal. 3:8) and "from whom, according to the flesh, Christ came, who is over all, the eternally blessed God" (Rom. 9:5).

The theme of Exodus is "I will take you as My people, and I will be your God" (Ex. 6:7). The first part of the book (chaps. 1–19) tells of the mighty deeds of God to create this nation by delivering it out of Egypt's house of bondage. In the second part (chaps. 20–40), God makes clear at Mount Sinai how this people is to acknowledge Him as their covenant God.

New Developments in Exodus

As a new element in Exodus, God selects Moses as the mediator of the covenant and as His spokesman (prophet) to the Israelites. Of the Levitical family of Kohath, the second son of Amram (Ex. 6:16–20), Moses will be God's "mouth," and God will teach him what he shall speak (4:12) in a way and to a degree unequalled by later spokesmen of God to Israel,[1] for "the Lord spoke to Moses face to face, as a man speaks to his friend" (Ex. 33:11). A weak and unwilling servant of God at first and not perfect in his obedience to Him later, Moses nevertheless interceded for his people, even offering his own life to save them: "Yet now, if You will forgive their sin—but if not, I pray, blot me out of Your book which You have written" (Ex. 32:32).

Another new and important element appears. A whole nation—no longer individuals and their families—now becomes the bearer of the covenant promises. In the past God had "negotiated" the covenant by speaking directly to the patriarchs. Now, as God's plan of salvation took on a national scope, it was necessary to speak to and to constitute the bearers of the covenant *as a nation*. Therefore, the covenant that God made at Sinai has been called appropriately "Israel's constitution."

A third new element is the frequent use of the words *holy* and *holiness*[2] to express and sum up the meaning of the principles of the covenant constitution. Israel is to be "a holy nation," that is, set apart as God's "special treasure . . . above all people" (19:5–6). They exist only to achieve the purposes to which God had consecrated them: to be "a kingdom of priests" (Ex. 19:6).

Israel is to be holy to the Lord individually and collectively, inwardly and outwardly. Because they are His own people, they will love Him and keep His commandments. They will have no other gods besides Him, and they will worship Him—at the times, at the places, in the manner, and through the mediators—as He prescribed.

The covenant on Mount Sinai constitutes Israel as a holy nation also in its human relationships. God has separated His people from all other nations and has determined their social, political,

---

[1] Indicative of his preeminent position, Moses' name occurs about 700 times in Exodus through Joshua.

[2] These significant terms are not found in Genesis and therefore are not associated with the earlier patriarchal covenant. In Genesis this concept appears only once in a verbal form: "God blessed the seventh day and sanctified it" (i.e., set it aside as holy; Gen. 2:3). In Exodus the adjective *holy* occurs 70 times, as well as often in a verbal form. Only Leviticus uses the adjective more frequently—92 times.

judicial, and economic framework. Within these Israel is to achieve His holy purposes. Some of the provisions were not unlike those of other nations of that day, but by adapting them, God hallowed Israel as His holy people.

As Israel was to be holy, separated and distinct from all other nations, so God is wholly different in an absolute way, "glorious in holiness" (15:11). His name is YAHWEH[3], "I AM WHO I AM" (3:14). He is beyond every dimension of yesterday, today, and tomorrow. Beyond the limits of human thinking, He is the great "I AM." He caused all of creation to be "in the beginning." "Before the mountains were brought forth, or ever You had formed the earth and the world, even from everlasting to everlasting, You are God" (Ps. 90:2). He is the God Almighty, who "appeared to Abraham, to Isaac, and to Jacob" (Ex. 6:3), manifesting that the universe and humanity were not autonomous but subject to His transcendent power and sovereign will. He could and did choose this people from among all peoples to achieve His purpose. Through their lives He staged for the world Act One of His drama of universal salvation by which the patriarchs themselves were saved.

Exodus raises the curtain on Act Two. To a nation holy to God He revealed His holy name in a manner in which He had not made Himself known to the patriarchs (6:3).[4] His name, therefore, is not merely an identifying appellation (i.e., Yahweh, "LORD"), but the sum total of His disclosure to all people by word and deed.[5]

At Mount Sinai God revealed His name to Israel in a more awesome manifestation of His holiness than the patriarchs had ever received. In "thunderings and lightnings, and a thick cloud" (19:16) He let it be known that humans cannot "break through to come up to the LORD, lest He break out against them" (19:24). He is holy, unapproachable, a devastating fire that consumes sin-

---

[3]The pronunciation of this name is uncertain. In ancient Hebrew, words were not spelled with vowels. Also, the oral pronunciation of Y-H-W-H was lost because the Jews refrained from speaking the holy Tetragrammaton (the four consonants) and substituted *Adonai* (Lord) wherever it occurred in the text. The form "Jehovah" is an artificial construction in which the Tetragrammaton is supplied with the Hebrew vowels from *Adonai*. Most scholars today agree that the name probably should be vocalized as "YAH-wey."

[4]This verse does not imply that "Yahweh," as an appellation, was not known previously. For example, Moses' mother's name, Jochebed (Ex. 6:20), is compounded of this proper noun for God.

[5]The translation "LORD" for the Hebrew Y-H-W-H does not reflect the full significance of the name. The explanation "I AM" connects it with the Hebrew *hayah*, "to be." God *is*—without any qualifications or restrictions. His lordship, therefore, is only one aspect of Him who is as no one else and nothing else is.

ful humanity.

But God also revealed at Sinai that His name is holy because He is "merciful and gracious, longsuffering, and abounding in goodness and truth, keeping mercy for thousands, forgiving iniquity and transgression and sin" (34:6-7). His covenant with Israel is the proclamation of His steadfast love and forgiving mercy.

In summary: The covenant at Sinai provides many forms and symbols unknown to the patriarchs. These forms and symbols both emphasize the need for the removal of sin as well as convey forgiveness by God's mercy. Thus, the holy God made Israel a holy nation to carry out His holy plan of redemption by the atonement of His own Son.

The Birth of a Nation (Chapters 1–19)

Exodus, the name of this Old Testament book, aptly describes that God made a holy nation out of an enslaved people by leading them out of bondage. The book is not an epic of Israel's glory, fortitude, heroism, or self-determination. Rather, it presents a most dismal and humiliating account of Israel's origin.

Oppressed by a foreign power "with hard bondage" and doomed to extinction by Pharaoh's decree of genocide (1:13–16), the Israelites responded to God's liberation only halfheartedly and reluctantly. Openly they resisted, saying, "Let us alone that we may serve the Egyptians," and they "would not heed Moses" (14:12; 6:9; cf. also 4:1; 5:19–21). After their deliverance by the mighty hand of God, they wanted to return to Egypt and murmured constantly (14:11; 15:24; 16:2–3; 17:2). Moses, too, was reluctant and took up the staff of leading the people only after God had prodded him into it and had overruled his excuses (3:11; 4:1, 10, 13; 6:30).

Thus, the Israelites became a free, holy people in spite of themselves—solely because "the Lord . . . set His love on you [and chose] you . . . because He [kept] the oath which He swore to your fathers" (Deut. 7:7–8).

THE DATE AND DURATION OF THE EXODUS EVENT

The main events of Exodus take place in a rather short span of time. Moses was 80 years old when he appeared before Pharaoh and demanded Israel's release. The liberation, the desert wanderings to Sinai, and the events at Sinai occupy no more than about a year's time.

The account of what happened at Mount Sinai, namely, the making of the covenant, begins in Exodus 19 and continues through Leviticus into Numbers 10. Then Israel resumes its march from Sinai to the Promised Land on the 20th day of the second month in the second year (Num. 10:11–12).

The date of the Exodus is a much debated issue. The controversy arises in part because of the lack of specific data in the Biblical record.[6] Scripture does not mention by name the Pharaohs at the time of the patriarchs or the Pharaohs of the oppression or of the Exodus. Furthermore, what happened to the Israelites during this time is not synchronized with specific events in the history of Egypt. In addition, Egyptian records make no mention of the Exodus period, nor is it likely they would—not something as damaging to national prestige as the escape of an enslaved people.

A study of the Biblical and recent archaeological data, however, favors the 15th century B.C. (ca. 1440) as the time when Israel left the house of bondage on the Nile.

The Sinai Covenant (Chapters 20–40)

Some scholars have compared Israel's confederacy to the amphictyonies of ancient Greece. In both societies homogeneous groups of people confederated under a mutual oath of allegiance to a common, recognized deity, by whom they pledge mutual support and defense—all in the confidence of divine sanction. But Israel's constitution contains far more elements than these.

Israel does not exist for its own national ends; God has created and organized this nation as a means to an end beyond itself. It is holy—chosen to be different from all nations—in order to bring to all nations what no nation could achieve for or of itself.

Nor does a national benefit of life with God accrue from a joint effort by Israel's 12 tribes. That was a gift from God by His forgiving mercy. Abraham received it before Israel came into being. The federation of his descendants likewise could only accept it by faith and trust.

Israel could claim only one distinction over other nations: God had chosen this nation to carry forward His plan of salvation for all nations; the woman's Seed was to be of the seed of Abraham

---

[6]Scripture gives a mixed description of how long the descendants of Israel were oppressed by the Egyptians. Cf. God's promise to Abraham: "They will afflict them four hundred years. . . . But in the fourth generation they shall return here" (Gen. 15:13, 16). H. C. Leupold suggests that the "four hundred years" is simply a round number, made more precise in Ex. 12:40, and that a generation was considered to be 100 years at that time (*Exposition of Genesis* [Columbus, Ohio: Wartburg Press, 1942], pp. 484, 486).

and Israel. "When the fullness of the time had come, God sent forth His Son, born of a woman [of Israel], born under the law, to redeem those who were under the law" (Gal. 4:4–5).

Nor did Israel's own thinking or doing produce its covenant constitution. Its preamble (Ex. 20:2) makes this clear: "I am the Lord your God, who brought you out of the land of Egypt, out of the house of bondage." All that Israel was to be and to do is based on what God is and has done. Only because He is merciful and forgives sin, only because He mercifully redeemed perishing slaves, can and does Israel have the privilege and responsibility to be what God wants it to be: a holy nation.

In the covenant God provided many ways and forms by which He reminds and assures Israel of its holy state of forgiveness. Ex. 20:1–17 contains the heart and core of God's law: The Ten Commandments. Ex. 20:22–23:33 contains "The Book of the Covenant," additional directions from the Lord. Ex. 24–40 presents God's prescriptions for worship as the enactment of its forgiveness and its uniqueness as a holy people.

THE TEN COMMANDMENTS/THE DECALOG (20:1–17)

Even as Israel exists by God's grace, so the covenant sets forth that Israel is *to give evidence* that it accepts this undeserved grace. The evidence is full devotion and complete obedience of faith. In its basic form, God's required response is summed up in 10 "words," the Ten Commandments. Their preeminence and permanence are indicated by the fact that God Himself engraved them on two tables (tablets) of stone.

God directs the Decalog to the individual: "You shall" and "You shall not." All that the Israelite is to think, say, and do in relationship to God and people is summarized in these brief but all-inclusive statements.

But these principles are to guide Israel equally as a nation. How they apply and the manner and the form in which Israel is to express them as a whole nation, individually and corporately, are set forth in the next 105 verses.

THE BOOK OF THE COVENANT (20:22–23:33)

Scripture itself provides the title for this section:

Moses wrote all the words of the Lord . . . [and] took the Book of the Covenant and read [it] in the hearing of the people. And they said, "All that the LORD has said we will do, and be obedient." And Moses took the blood [of the sacrificed oxen], sprinkled it on the people, and said, "Behold, the blood of the covenant which the LORD has made with you according to all these words." (24:4, 7–8)

These words have also been called the covenant "code," but they are not strictly codified according to topics. The laws are not even separated into secular and religious/moral groupings, as might be done today.[7] This mixture exists because Israel was constituted as a theocracy. God Himself legislated how Israel—in all areas of its inner and outer, individual and collective life—will live as the instrument of His life-giving purposes.

Therefore, the Book of the Covenant, like the Decalog, begins with an ordinance by which Israel is to acknowledge God's total and undivided claim on His people. By sacrifices on an altar, erected according to His specifications, they are to remember that He has "talked with you from heaven" and that He "will come to you and . . . bless you" in their obedience to Him (20:22–24).

The bulk of the covenant code tells how God wants Israel to be holy to Him in areas usually defined as political, social, economic, and judicial.

Even though the multiplicity and details of these ancient laws may bog down today's reader, and though they no longer bind the new covenant in Christ any more than do the ceremonial prescriptions for Israel, yet these laws are the "shadow of things to come" (Col. 2:17), "written for our learning" (Rom. 15:4). The total commitment that God claimed from His people of the old covenant impresses on the free people of the new covenant that no area, phase, or detail of life is purely secular or profane. The redeemed are holy to the Lord: "Whether you eat or drink, or whatever you do, do all to the glory of God" (1 Cor. 10:31).

THE COVENANT ENACTED IN WORSHIP (CHAPTERS 24–40)

The covenant code (chaps. 20–23) is the nucleus of the Mosaic law. On succeeding days at Mount Sinai God added to it by amplification and elaboration. These more detailed specifications fill almost all the remaining chapters of Exodus (chaps. 24–40, as well as Leviticus and the first part of Numbers).

Worship of God in rites and sacrifices (mentioned only in general terms in the Book of the Covenant and described more precisely in subsequent chapters) expresses and actualizes God's covenant relationship with Israel. Therefore, the rites and sacri-

---

[7]For example, in 23:14–17 God specifies that Israel's national holidays are to be holy "feast" days: "The Feast of Unleavened Bread, . . . the Feast of Harvest, . . . and the Feast of Ingathering, which is at the end of the year. . . . Three times in the year all your males shall appear before the Lord GOD."

53

fices are to be performed in a holy place equipped for that purpose (the tabernacle) and by a holy personnel (the priesthood).

The Tabernacle

Two basic aspects of the tabernacle stand out. First, Israel is not to design its own worship center. God Himself showed Moses in detail "the pattern of the tabernacle and the pattern of all its furnishings" (Ex. 25:9; cf also 25:40; 26:30; 27:8).[8] To show that these instructions were followed, Scripture gives a long account of the building of the tabernacle (chaps. 35–39) and its first use (chap. 40).

Second, the entire plan of the tabernacle signified its use as a "sanctuary," that is, a holy place (25:8; cf. also 36:1, 6). The holy God can be approached only by worshipers who accept His forgiving mercy. The tabernacle will be God's dwelling place where He will commune with a people cleansed of unholiness.

The innermost part of the tabernacle, therefore, is the "Holy of Holies," that is, the most holy of holy places. Here stood the Ark of the Testimony containing the tables of the law. The golden lid of this chest was the "mercy seat" (25:17). The high priest sprinkled on it the atoning blood of the sacrifice as a covering for and atonement of the breaking of the law. Thus, the mercy seat became the place of God's presence among His people. Here He dwelt between the cherubim in the mystery of His divine condescension, gathering His people to Himself at the tabernacle, the "tent of meeting."

The "Holy Place," that part of the tabernacle through which the high priest passed to enter the Holy of Holies, also emphasized the importance of holiness in worship. Only the priests, those who sanctified the people, could enter its precincts. As representatives of the people in their communion with God, the priests burned incense daily on an altar of incense (30:1–10), placed the bread of the Presence (showbread) on a table (25:23–30; 26:35), and tended the lamps of the seven-armed candelabrum (25:31–40; 26:35).

Even the court of the tabernacle was a holy place. Here stood the altar of burnt offering. On it the priests burned the sacrificial animals by which the people were ritually sanctified for communion with God and on which they offered their thanks and praise.

---

[8]This portable tabernacle also served as a basic model for the temple of Solomon (1 Kings 6).

The Tabernacle

The Priests

The public administration of the general worship rites of a holy people in a holy tabernacle was restricted to a holy (i.e., specially designated) group: the tribe of Levi. And within this tribe, only Aaron and his descendants are sanctified or consecrated for the specific function of the priesthood proper (28:1). But not even all priests are permitted to perform all the rites. Aaron was to be "holy to the Lord" in a special way—as *the* priest or High Priest. Only he and the firstborn among his descendants, for example, could enter the Holy of Holies.[9] And to emphasize their holy functions, all officiants in the sanctuary are to wear "holy garments" (28:2–4; 39:1–30) and to be consecrated in an ordination ceremony (29:1–37; 40:12–15).

Amid all these specifics about holy worship (between the directions, chaps. 24–31, and their performance, chaps. 34–40) is inserted (chaps. 32–34) perhaps the most unholy and humiliating account of Israel's early life: its breaking of the covenant by the worship of the golden calf at the same time that the covenant was established. That God forgave them testifies clearly that the God of the covenant truly is a God of mercy and forgiveness.

· · · · ·

All that God did for and through Israel of old was above all prophetic history. It pointed forward to the consummation of His eternal plan of salvation through His Son, Jesus Christ.

The exodus from Egypt and the making of the covenant at Mount Sinai are events of history, both Israel's history as well as the history of the people of the new covenant—"a chosen generation, a royal priesthood, a holy nation, His [God's] own special people" (1 Peter 2:9). The latter became God's people just as did the first—not by merit but by the saving and forgiving mercy of God.

The purpose of both covenants is the same: that God's people of all ages may "proclaim the praises of Him who called you out of darkness into His marvelous light" and in order to "be holy in all your conduct" (1 Peter 2:9; 1:15).

The continuous nature of the covenant is witnessed on a holy mountain where "Moses and Elijah . . . appeared in glory and spoke of His decease [Greek: His exodus] which He was about to accomplish [Greek: fulfill] at Jerusalem" (Luke 9:30–31). In His death Jesus entered once and for all into the Most Holy Place,

---

[9]Later the nonpriestly Levites, i.e., those not of Aaron's family, are designated to be "ministers" of the priests (cf. Num. 3–4).

sprinkling not the blood of goats and calves but His own blood, thus securing an eternal redemption (Heb. 9:12). It is the blood of the new covenant because it is God's yes and amen of the fulfillment of His old covenant promises.

The old covenant was God's signature of promise; the new covenant validates the promise.

5. Leviticus

Leviticus, the shortest book of the Pentateuch, may seem the longest because of a profusion of seemingly irrelevant cultic detail. But the book's importance remains because, as part of the covenant, it provides fuller instruction for Israel's relationship to God. Rather than introduce basically new or different instructions, the book elaborates, applies, and implements principles already set forth in Exodus.

God chose to present the Law as successive and ever-widening concentric circles begun in Exodus. The Decalog and its preamble (Ex. 20) are at the center. The Book of the Covenant (Ex. 21–24) constitutes the next circle. The remaining chapters of Exodus widen the scope to the tabernacle and priesthood. Leviticus provides still another circle of specifications.

Although the multitude of individual directives in Leviticus may seem bewildering, keep in mind the whole picture—an entire complex of legislation designed to instruct the Israelites on how they are to respond to God's covenant of undeserved goodness and grace. Its recurring theme (as throughout the Pentateuch) is "You shall be holy, for I the LORD your God am holy" (Lev. 19:2; cf. 11:45; Ex. 19:6).[1] To be a holy nation, Israel, inwardly and outwardly, is to be *separated from* all that defiles and *dedicated to* God by an undefiled life of purity.

These requirements provide a general structure to the book. Holiness requires, first of all, cleansing from sin by a sacrificial atonement. Such a holy people then expresses its desire for reconciliation with God and enjoys the resultant communion with God by offering various offerings. A holy people also will give evidence of its dedication to God by observing God's ordinances for a life that is consecrated to Him according to His will. These themes provide the following outline:

Chapters 1–10: The worship rites to symbolize and actualize Israel's access to God and fellowship with Him.

Chapters 11–16: The prerequisites for worship:
  A. Abstinence from and removal of outward defilement (chaps. 11–15);
  B. Cleansing by atonement from the pollution of sin (chap. 16).

---

[1]The word *holy* and its derivatives occur some 130 times in this book.

Chapters 17–27: The worship of God in a life of total consecration and obedience to God's will.

Three Events: Leviticus also contains three historical events that highlight obedience (and disobedience) to the covenant: (1) Moses, following the prescriptions in Ex. 29, consecrates those who are to serve in the tabernacle (chaps. 8–9). (2) Nadab and Abihu, two sons of Aaron, fail to follow the directions of sacrifice and are consumed by fire (10:1–7). (3) A man is punished (stoned) for violating the law against blasphemy (24:10–23).

The Worship Rites (Chapters 1–10)

Leviticus begins with a historical and logical connection to the end of Exodus: "The Lord called to Moses, and spoke to him from the tabernacle of meeting" (Lev. 1:1). The tabernacle had been completed, and the ministers for its worship had been appointed and equipped with vestments. Chapters 1–7 of Leviticus proceed to enumerate the sacrifices of the tabernacle, and chapters 8–10 describe the ordination of the worship personnel and the dedication of the tabernacle itself.

In chapters 1–7, five kinds of sacrifices are described:

1. Burnt Offerings	1:2–17	6:8–13
2. Grain Offerings	2:1–16	6:14–23
3. Peace Offerings	3:1–17	7:11–34
4. Sin Offerings	4:1–35	6:24–30
5. Trespass Offerings	5:14–6:7	7:1–10

All but the grain offering required the slaying of an animal. Although people brought these blood offerings to the Lord, God required them as His way to instruct and assure His people that they are acceptable to Him by way of the substitutionary shedding of blood. The worshiper accepted this fact by laying his hand on the victim "to make atonement for him" (1:4; 3:8; 4:4). The grain offering symbolized, made possible, conveyed, and assured to the worshiper an accomplished, active fellowship with God.

Holiness, the Prerequisite for Worship (Chapters 11–16)

Chapters 11–15

This part stresses, first of all, outward cleanliness as a prerequisite for worship. Those people are clean who have avoided or removed physical contaminations.

Moses describes various contaminations. Unholiness results from eating animals that are declared unclean (chap. 11; in some cases, hygienic reasons for avoidance may be involved.) After childbirth, a woman can "come into a sanctuary [only after] the days of her purification are fulfilled" (chap. 12; since procreation and childbearing are legitimate functions, purification apparently called attention to one's innate and congenital depravity: original sin.) Chapters 13–14 exclude lepers from worship as well as from living among the healthy community. The affected person "shall dwell alone; his dwelling shall be outside the camp" (13:46; again, hygienic purposes seem to be involved.) A final section (chap. 15) declares that sexual emissions and secretions make men and women unclean and unfit for worship. (The tie to original sin again may be involved.)

The main reason for these distinctions between clean and unclean may not be anything as "practical" as hygiene but simply that God was emphasizing the uniqueness of His people. The statement at the conclusion of chapter 15 applies to all the regulations: "Thus you shall separate the children of Israel from their uncleanness, lest they die in their uncleanness when they defile My tabernacle that is among them" (15:31).

Chapter 16

But more than elimination of merely physical or outward defilement is required for access to and fellowship with God. For the people to be holy, completely "clean" before the Lord, able to appear in His presence and to commune with Him, atonement must be made. The people must be cleansed of all their sins (v. 30). How such total holiness comes to Israel is graphically and impressively portrayed in the ceremonies of the Day of Atonement.

All forms of Israel's worship climax in the drama of that day. The offerings and sacrifices mentioned in chapters 1–6, as well as those of every Sabbath and feast day, have validity and meaning only if Israel accepts what is here offered so comprehensively and absolutely: the forgiveness of sins.

Three basic principles emerge. First, atonement (blood payment) must be made because sin incurs God's wrath and punishment. Second, atonement is not effected by Israel but is *made for* the people. A bull and a goat are slain in the people's stead, and the sacrificial, substitutionary blood is sprinkled on the mercy seat by the high priest, who enters the Holy of Holies only on this day of the year. Third, God's forgiveness is full and without reservation:

> Aaron [and any subsequent high priest] shall lay both his hands on the head of [another] live goat, confess over it all the iniquities of the children of Israel, and all their transgressions, concerning all their sins, putting them on the head of the goat, and shall

send it away into the wilderness. (16:21)

Borne away by the "scapegoat" (escape goat), the sins are gone forever.

The Holy Life As Worship (Chapters 17–27)

Holiness has another aspect. More than eliminating every unclean thing and defilement, holiness (on the positive side) includes living in obedience under God, the corollary of being chosen by God. Therefore, this section (particularly chaps. 17–27), has been called the "Holiness Code."[2]

As in former legislation of the covenant, a profusion of laws is here enacted that today are classified as political, social, ethical, dietary, cultic, and ceremonial. Again, some of these appear odd and even arbitrary, while others are designed to prevent the Israelites from acting "according to the doings of the land of Egypt . . . [and] of the land of Canaan" (18:3; cf., for example, chap. 20). Disobedience, including sin against people, is sin against God's holiness. But God gives only this comprehensive reason for the promulgation of the laws: "You shall be holy, for I the LORD your God am holy. . . . I am the LORD your God" (19:1, 34). And Israel has only one motive for keeping these laws: the need to respond to God for all that He has done to redeem and consecrate Israel as His people.

In the first set of prescriptions (chap. 17), God stresses and explains the significance attached to the shedding of sacrificial blood: "The life of all flesh is its blood" (17:14; cf. verse 11). When it is shed in sacrifice, a life is offered in substitution for the life of a person that is forfeit by sin. The giver of life has ordained, "I have *given* it [the blood] to you . . . to make atonement for your souls; for it is the blood that makes atonement for the soul" (17:11, emphasis added).[3] Israel is to indicate its acceptance of God's provision for atonement by observing two ceremonial ordinances. (1) The sacrificial animals (ox, lamb, goat) may be eaten only when they are slain "at the door of the tabernacle of meeting" as peace offerings to the Lord (17:1–7). (2) "You shall not eat the blood of any flesh" (17:10–16).

---

[2]Leviticus is more than a manual for priests (as some have claimed). As the channel of communication for the Holiness Code, Moses is to relay these injunctions and sayings to the people of Israel. Only chapters 21–22 are directed exclusively to the priests, to Aaron and his sons.

[3]The new covenant writer to the Hebrews reiterates that point: "Without shedding of blood there is no remission" (9:22).

Chapter 18

A holy people will also avoid defiling marriage and sex relations, lest by following "the doings" of Egypt and Canaan, those who so sin "be cut off from among their people" (v. 29).

Chapter 19

This chapter gives precepts for holy living in a wide range of areas—worship, ceremony, ethics, morals, social and economic standards. The intermingling of duties to God and duties to people emphasizes that both tables of the Law are integral to the covenant.

Chapter 20

God reemphasizes that Israel cannot presume to disregard the requirements of the covenant. If the people refuse to be holy under a holy God, their self-made separation shall be enforced by death or by being cut off from the community.

Chapters 21–22

God sets the requirements for holiness of the priests above and beyond that of the people. Just as Israel is separated from the nations, so the priests (in their sanctuary duties) are separate from and representatives of the whole nation.

Chapters 23–25

Israel is directed to express its holiness by regularly setting aside days for "feasts" and "holy convocation."

First, every seventh day is a Sabbath, or day of rest (23:3; cf. Ex. 20:8–11; 31:13–17). And on the first day of the seventh month, Israel shall observe "a sabbath-rest" (Lev. 23:23–25, sometimes called the Feast of Trumpets) to mark the beginning of a "civil" year.

Second, on three days of the year, every male Israelite shall appear before the sanctuary. These pilgrimage feasts, though initiated in Exodus, are elaborated in Leviticus.

1. The Passover, to commemorate the deliverance from Egypt and "the passing over" (redemption) of the firstborn of Israel. On the next seven days, no leavened bread should be eaten (the Feast of Unleavened Bread). Since it "shall be a statute forever throughout your generations in all your dwellings" (23:14), this latter feast continued as a ceremony after Israel was established in Canaan: the dedication of the first sheaf of early grain, recognizing God's blessing on the soil (23:6–14; cf. Ex. 12:11–20).
2. The Feast of Weeks, or Pentecost—the 50th day after the

Passover (Lev. 23:15–22; cf. Ex. 23:16; 34:22). Also called the Feast of Harvest, this too honored God's blessing on the soil.

3. The Feast of Tabernacles, also called the Feast of Ingathering (Lev. 23:33–43; Ex. 23:16). Israel was to live in tabernacles (tentlike structures) as a reminder of its desert wandering and to rejoice over the completion of the harvests.

These chapters include supplementary directives regarding the things of the sanctuary (24:1–9) and extend the Sabbath rest to holy years: every seventh year was a sabbatical year, and after seven sabbatical years came the Year of Jubilee (so-called because it is ushered in by blowing a horn—Hebrew: *yobel*). Observing these years reminds Israel again that all aspects of its life—agrarian, social and economic—are part of holy living to the Lord (chap. 25).

Chapter 26

This chapter restates that obedience to all these statutes results in blessing, while disobedience brings punishment and retribution.

Chapter 27

Leviticus closes with stipulations regarding vows and the dedication to the Lord of persons and things not specifically required in the Law.

Leviticus: Outmoded or Relevant?

The demand for holiness did not end with the old covenant. Consider just a few passages from the new covenant:

Present your members as slaves of righteousness for holiness. (Rom. 6:19)

Present your bodies a living sacrifice, holy, acceptable to God. (Rom. 12:1)

Let us cleanse ourselves from all filthiness of the flesh and spirit, perfecting holiness in the fear of God. (2 Cor. 7:1)

We should be holy and without blame before Him. (Eph. 1:4)

[He] called us with a holy calling, not according to our works, but according to His own purpose and grace. (2 Tim. 1:9)

As He who called you is holy, you also be holy in all your conduct. (1 Peter 1:15)

In fact, were these passages (and many others from the New Testament) encountered in Leviticus, they would not be considered foreign elements.

Like Israel, the people of the new covenant must be holy in order to be in communion with God, and they must give evidence of that communion in holy worship and holy lives. Though many of the laws in Leviticus no longer apply (Gal. 3:19–25), the book (indeed, all the Law) still provides profitable instruction in holy living (Rom 7:6; 12:1–2; 2 Tim. 3:16–17).

But since unholiness awaits God's people at every corner of life, they (like Israel) must be *accounted* holy:

> For it pleased the Father . . . to reconcile all things to Himself, . . . having made peace through the blood of His cross. . . .
> He has reconciled [you] in the body of His flesh through death, to present you holy, and blameless, and above reproach in His sight. (Col. 1:19–23)

This reconciliation is once and for all; every sin becomes contemporary with it and is atoned. The Lamb of God, slaughtered 20 centuries ago, gave benefit for sins committed today as well as for Israel's sins long ago, for "it is not possible that the blood of bulls and goats should take away sins" (Heb. 10:4).

The sacrifices of the Old Testament have been abrogated because they pointed forward to the blood of Christ, who has come. Yet even the New Testament believer (who is, at the same time, a sinner with "natural" thinking) needs to read of them and hear again and again the underlying theology:

Sin is not a trivial matter. Every breaking of God's will, including unwitting sin, has deadly consequences.

People can do nothing to make themselves acceptable to God. Their forfeited lives can be redeemed only by an atonement, a substitution, that God has "given on the altar."

People daily need to seek the forgiving mercy of God.

Total redemption calls forth a total response and commitment to God. Holy living is living wholly to God. "Therefore you shall be perfect, just as your Father in heaven is perfect" (Matt. 5:48).

The Israelites of old may not have understood or anticipated all this—or needed to. They had faith in the promised deliverance of God, a deliverance fulfilled in the coming of the Deliverer, the Lamb of God, who was offered as the final, perfect sacrifice. They received forgiveness and salvation through their trust in the promised deliverance. Whenever Israel brought sacrifices to confess sins and beg forgiveness, God accepted the sacrifices and used them as a channel of His forgiving mercy. Of this Luther says very fitly and decisively:

> We treat of the forgiveness of sins in two ways. First, how it is achieved and won. Second, how it is distributed and given to us. Christ has achieved it on the cross, it is true. But he has not distributed or given it on the cross. . . . He has distributed and given it through the Word, as also in the gospel, where it is preached. He has won it once for all on the cross. But the distribution takes place continuously, before and after, from the beginning of the world. For inasmuch as he had determined once to achieve it, it made no difference to him whether he distributed it before or after [the cross], through his Word, as can easily be proved from Scripture. . . . When we consider the application of the forgiveness, we are not dealing with a particular time, but find that it has taken place from the beginning of the world. So St. John in the Book of Revelation [13:8] says that the Lamb of God was slain before the foundation of the world.[4]

Thus, by God's design the sacrifices pointed beyond themselves to the Sacrifice by which the old sacrifices were valid as means of God's grace.

• • • • •

Reading Leviticus is not an act of penance, but it may lead to repentance. It should drum into modern ears the inviolability of God's laws within every detail, within every area of one's relationship to Him and to other people. People today too are unholy unless they love their neighbor as themselves (Lev. 19:18; cf. Matt. 22:39 and parallel passages). Leviticus teaches what Jesus taught: "You shall be perfect, just as your Father in heaven is perfect" (Matt. 5:48).

The book should be read in a day that has lost the sense of the holy; for, as St. Paul wrote:

> Shall we continue in sin that grace may abound? Certainly not! How shall we who died to sin live any longer in it? Or do you not know that as many of us as were baptized into Christ Jesus were baptized into His death? Therefore we were buried with Him through baptism into death, that just as Christ was raised from the dead by the glory of the Father, even so we also should walk in newness of life. (Rom. 6:1-4)

---

[4]Martin Luther, "Against the Heavenly Prophets in the Matter of Images and Sacraments," Part II, trans. Conrad Bergendoff, in *Church and Ministry II,* ed. *Helmut T. Lehmann; Luther's Works,* American Edition, vol. 40 (Philadelphia: Muhlenberg Press, 1958): 213–15. Used by permission of Augsburg Fortress.

6. Numbers

Numbers, like Leviticus, adds another concentric circle of covenant legislation to the core provisions of Exodus. The pattern of blended legislation and history remains the same, but history takes a more prominent place in Numbers than in Leviticus, and the laws are more incidental and largely occasioned by circumstances.

In contrast to Leviticus (at Sinai and covering just a few months), the events in Numbers take place at more than 40 places and during 38 years. In a general way, Leviticus tells us what God *said* to the covenant nation, and Numbers (more like Exodus) what God *did* to bring Israel to the Land of Promise. As a result, its legislative sections are interwoven into the historical narrative. In fact, this book contains some of the most dramatic events of the Old Testament.

The Narrative Sections of Numbers

The reader readily recognizes in Numbers its progressive outline of events. By the end of the book, Israel is in the Plains of Moab, across the Jordan River from Jericho, poised for the final step of crossing the river to conquer Canaan. Exodus 19:2 gave the previous progress report: They had "come to the Desert of Sinai, and . . . camped there before the mountain" (Ex. 19:2). Numbers provides the intervening events.

OVERVIEW OF THE BOOK

Numbers begins at Sinai with a census and with preparations (marching orders) for the journey to the Promised Land (1:2–10:10).

Israel left Mount Sinai (10:11–13) and marched northward to Canaan but was prevented from immediately attaining the goal. As punishment for rebelling against God, Israel was sentenced to 40 years (2 completed plus 38 more years) of wandering in the desert.

Although the Israelites continued to rebel against their God-appointed leaders, after 38 years they arrived again at the point of their previous northernmost advance, Kadesh (20:1).

From Kadesh (20:22), in the 40th year of the Exodus, they skirted the lands of Edom and Moab (21:4), moved northwest into the Plains of Moab (Amorite territory along the Jordan River north of Moab), and conquered it (21:21–25).

Numbers concludes with Israel in the Plains of Moab.

THE EVENTS AT SINAI (1:1–10:10)

Numbering Israel

The book begins with God's order to Moses: "Take a census of all the congregation of the children of Israel, by their families, by their fathers' houses, according to the number of names, every male individually, from twenty years old and above—all who are able to to go war in Israel" (Num. 1:2–3). In addition to effectively organizing for the battle march to Canaan, the census brought with it two other benefits:

A systematic means to defray construction cost of the tabernacle by the payment of "half a shekel, according to the shekel of the sanctuary, for everyone included in the numbering from twenty years old and above, for six hundred and three thousand, five hundred and fifty men" (Ex. 38:26; cf. Num. 2:32).

The opportunity to assign the Levites ("not numbered among [the army of] the children of Israel" [Num. 2:33], but still counted) specific duties and positions at the tabernacle "by their fathers' houses, by their families" (3:15).

Observations on These Census Figures: Since the number of men old enough for military duty was 603,550, the total for the entire people must have been in excess of two million. Such a large group certainly could not have moved about and survived in the desert except by direct intervention of God, and some of His miraculous means are specifically mentioned in this book.

These figures are not epic embellishments or poetic devices typical of a national saga. There is no reason to suppose that this account, factual about Israel's unheroic behavior, should resort to poetic license to save Israel's (or God's) honor by inflating so prosaic a matter as simple statistics.

Attempts have been made to reduce these large numbers to be compatible with the prevailing conditions and circumstances. But these proposed solutions should not be regarded as valid if they are designed to cast doubt on the miraculous acts of God to sustain His people in the desert.[1]

---

[1]For a more detailed discussion of this topic, cf. *Concordia Self-Study Commentary*, pp. 103–04.

Ready to March

Chapters 1–10 could have been included in Leviticus. The setting is still Mount Sinai, and the events are linked to the tabernacle and its building.[2] The note in 7:1, "when Moses had finished setting up the tabernacle," picks up the action from Exodus 40:17, when "in the first month of the second year, on the first day of the month, . . . the tabernacle was raised up."

Already from Num. 1 one expects new developments. A new movement forward is in the making. Now Israel has a sanctuary—a nerve center—and this requires a physical orientation around it.

The time is at hand for Israel to move the portable tabernacle for the first time. The Levites, purified for the dismantling, carrying, and reassembling of the tabernacle,[3] are about to receive their procedural instructions.

The first order to break camp and to advance was about to be given—not by Moses but by God, for "at the command of the LORD they remained encamped, and at the command of the LORD they journeyed" (9:23). Recall that "on the day that the tabernacle was raised up [the first time], the cloud covered the tabernacle, the tent of the Testimony" (9:15). Thus, when Israel would see the cloud "taken up from above the tabernacle," it was to set out from Mount Sinai and proceed till the place "where the cloud settled" (9:17).

The tabernacle was literally the center of Israel's camping and marching. From now on, the tribes were to be grouped in a square about the sanctuary. As the inner square, the tribe of Levi surrounded the tabernacle on all sides (2:17).[4] The other tribes extended from them, three on each of the four sides, each side under the leadership of one of its tribes (2:18–31).[5]

Israel is drawn up at attention, as it were, ready for the signal. The trumpets "for calling the assembly and for directing the movement of the camps" (as well as for other purposes) had been made

---

[2]Num. 7 reports an additional feature of the dedication not mentioned in Exodus: The leaders of each tribe, on 12 successive days, brought their identical offerings to the Lord (7:2–3, 11). Chapter 8 reports on the lighting of the lamps (vv. 1–4) and the purification of the Levites (vv. 5–26), the latter presumably after the consecration of the priests (Ex. 40).

[3]After the tabernacle is set up again, the Levites are to function also in areas of service, as delineated in Ex. 3–4.

[4]Aaron and his sons were placed in front of the ark to indicate their preeminence within the tribe; they alone were the priests. The remainder of the Levites formed the other three sides of this square around the tabernacle.

[5]No reason is given for the grouping or for the prominence assigned to the four leader tribes: Judah, Reuben, Ephraim, and Dan.

by Moses and were ready to be sounded by the priests (10:1–10). But one more event is mentioned as significant at this point.

Seven days before the Israelites left Sinai, "they kept the Passover" (9:1–5). It was the second anniversary of the first Passover in Egypt.[6] It seems to say that Israel is again ready and alert, as it was in Egypt, for the signal to move forward. Leaving Mount Sinai, therefore, was like another exodus—this one beginning the second great phase in the fulfillment of God's covenant: setting out as a theocratic nation toward Canaan. The conquest should follow in short order.

From Sinai to Kadesh (10:11–14:45)

Israel responded to the divine signal to leave Mount Sinai in the assigned formation. It was "on the twentieth day of the second month, in the second year" (10:11). The next major stop was to be near Kadesh in the Wilderness of Paran (10:12), the edge of Canaan.

But Israel had not left its sullen spirit and rebelliousness at Mount Sinai. In fact, the closer they came to Canaan, the more violent their murmuring and resistance became. On the way, they complained about their general misfortunes (11:1–3) and particularly about the lack of variety in their food compared with the fleshpots of Egypt (11:4–6). Moses often had interceded for his people (e.g., 11:2), but this time he gave up unheroically under their perversity and ingratitude (11:10–15). So the Lord lightened Moses' responsibility by providing 70 elders from the people as his helpers. God also provided Israel with meat in the form of quail but still punished Israel for its rebellion. "While the meat was still between their teeth, before it was chewed, the wrath of the LORD was aroused against the people . . . with a very great plague" (11:33).

Not even Aaron and Miriam remained loyal. They let jealousy provoke them to rebel against Moses' leadership (chap. 12).

In spite of it all, the people did arrive in the vicinity of Kadesh (12:16). During the stay there, 12 spies were sent into Canaan. Their report provoked more murmuring and finally open mutiny: "Let us select a leader and return to Egypt" (14:4). This crisis resulted in a most decisive turning point in Israel's history. Again Moses interceded for his people, and again God was moved not to exterminate the entire nation on the spot. But as a punishment

---

[6]Neither the previous anniversary nor any observance of this festival is recorded for the remainder of Israel's sojourn in the desert.

for their uprising, Israel was barred from entering the Promised Land at that time and condemned to wander in the wilderness for a total of 40 years. The obstinacy of the people reached a new height when, after the Lord had forbidden it, the people tried to enter Canaan anyway.

THE LOST YEARS OF WANDERING (CHAPTERS 15—19)

The title of this section could be "From Kadesh to Kadesh," for after 38 years of travel in various parts of the Sinai peninsula, Israel is reported again coming back into the Wilderness of Zin and staying at Kadesh (20:1).

This long page in Israel's history is left almost blank, and the only two recorded events besmirch it. First, a man was caught breaking the Sabbath (15:32–36). Second, the Levite Korah, along with Dathan, Abiram and On (Reubenites), revolted against Moses as leader and against Aaron as high priest and were annihilated (chap. 16). "As a sign against the rebels" and as a reminder of God's choice of Aaron, the latter's sprouted staff was to be kept in the tabernacle in perpetuity (chap. 17).

FROM KADESH ON THE WAY TO MOAB (CHAPTERS 20—21)

Ending with Israel ready to enter Canaan, chapters 21–36 present in chronological order the events of 40th year. But for Israel's rebellion, it might have been the third.

Chapters 21–22 relate Israel's march from Kadesh to Canaan via a detour around the territories immediately to the north, Edom and Moab. On the way, at Mount Hor, Aaron died, and Eleazar (his son) succeeded him (20:22–29).

While still in the Negev area (south of Canaan), Israel faced and overcame the opposition of a Canaanite King, Arad (21:1–3), an indication of the battles still to come.

On its way around Edom, Israel again murmured about the lack of food and water: "Our soul loathes this worthless bread." Fiery serpents bit the people and many died, but those lived who looked at the bronze serpent set on a pole by Moses (21:4–9).[7]

Once northeast of Moab, Israel moved northwest to conquer the Amorite kingdom of Sihon and Og north of the Arnon River (21:10–35).

---

[7]The bronze serpent remained in existence until King Hezekiah destroyed it (ca. 715 B.C.) when it was being used as a snake god named Nehushtan (2 Kings 18:4).

The Exodus

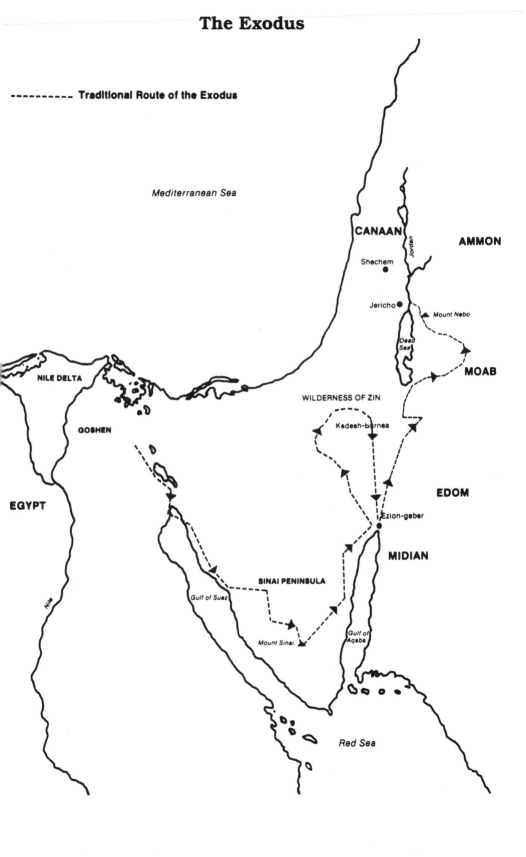

Traditional Route of the Exodus

Mediterranean Sea

CANAAN

AMMON

Shechem

Jordan

Jericho

Mount Nebo

NILE DELTA

Dead Sea

MOAB

GOSHEN

WILDERNESS OF ZIN

Kadesh-barnea

EGYPT

EDOM

Ezion-geber

MIDIAN

Gulf of Suez

SINAI PENINSULA

Nile

Mount Sinai

Gulf of Aqaba

Red Sea

In the Plains of Moab (Chapters 22–33)

The territory taken from the Amorite kings is called the Plains of Moab. Perhaps it was the northern extension of Moab or originally part of Moab. While Israel was encamped there, the following incidents took place:

Balaam (Chapters 22–24)

In this story, one of the most remarkable of the Old Testament, God uses a heathen diviner to prophesy about the Messiah.

Engaged by Balak (king of the Moabites) to curse Israel, Balaam instead blessed Israel in four highly poetic and prophetic utterances that climaxed in prophesying that "a Star shall come out of Jacob, a Scepter shall rise out of Israel" (24:17). These prophesies found a first step toward fulfillment in the kingdom of David, but their final and full meaning appeared when a star shone over Bethlehem and when the King of the Jews held in His bound hand a reed scepter and died with a crown of thorns on His head so that His kingdom might come.

Balaam provides an interesting study of human weakness and duplicity. Though outwardly obedient, inwardly Balaam was self-centered, obstinate, and greedy. His ignominious death was not undeserved (31:8). Yet God used this contrary-minded man (even his animal) to communicate His word—whether Balaam agreed with and understood the message or not.

Harlotry (Chapter 25)

The Midianites, related to Israel through Moses' marriage and closely associated with the Moabites and their idols, proved too enticing. Israel succumbed to spiritual harlotry (unfaithful idolatry) and to physical harlotry in the lascivious worship of the Baal of Peor. Decisive, violent action by Phinehas, grandson of Aaron, saved the day. He was rewarded with "a covenant of an everlasting priesthood, because he was zealous for his God, and made atonement for the children of Israel" (v. 13).

Another Census (Chapter 26)

Thirty-eight years had elapsed since the fist census. A whole generation had passed from the scene. Changes in the composition of the tribes had occurred as a result of plagues and other forms of God's punishment.

Now Israel was ready to take possession of its inheritance, and the land was to be allotted according to tribal strength (vv. 52–56). The age of those counted was again to be 20 years, the age of military duty. Some tribes (e.g., the Levites) remained the same in size. Some increased. Simeon's count was down by more than 37,000. But Israel's total of 601,730 is remarkably close to the 603,550 of the first census.

Joshua Named Successor (27:12–23)

Moses was barred from entering the Promised Land, "for in the Wilderness of Zin, during the strife of the congregation, you rebelled against My command to hallow Me at the waters before their eyes" (v. 14; cf. 20:1–13). So the Lord directed Moses to commission his successor, Joshua. But God would not communicate His will directly through Joshua as He did through Moses; instead, it would come "by the judgment of the Urim" (27:21).

Vengeance on the Midianites (Chapter 31)

Because of the Midianite seduction of Israel at Baal Peor (chap. 25), the Israelites carry out God's command to "harass the Midianites, and attack them" (25:17). Chapter 31 tells how this was carried out and the ensuing problems because the female Midianites were not killed but taken alive.

The Allotment of Land East of the Jordan River (Chapter 32)

The tribes of Reuben, Gad, and half of Manasseh were permitted to occupy the territory taken from the Amorite kings, Sihon and Og. But they were required to promise assistance in the conquest of Canaan west across the Jordan.

A Summary of the Journey from Egypt (Chapter 33)

Because "Moses wrote down the starting points of their journeys at the command of the LORD" (v. 2), this chapter might be called the log book of the journey from Egypt to the Plains of Moab. It lists some 40 places of encampment along the route. Some of them had been mentioned in Exodus and Numbers (cf. especially Num. 21:10–20), but most were not. No places of encampment, for example, had been given for the 38 years of punitive wandering from Kadesh (13:26) to Kadesh (20:1). Some of these stations cannot be definitely identified today, but their importance lies in testifying to the historicity of the Exodus, not in their exact location.

The Legislative Sections of Numbers

Laws and directives of all kinds are scattered throughout Numbers.

Old Laws

Many legislative sections contain directives already given in Exodus and Leviticus (cf. Num. 28:6: "ordained at Mount Sinai") but are here elaborated and their meaning deepened. Among these are:

The removal of unclean persons from the camp (5:1–4) and restitution for wrongs done (5:5–10).
The laws of sacrifice, emphasizing the meal offerings (chap. 15).
The rights and duties of the Levites (chap. 18).
The laws regarding offerings on established feast days and regarding vows (chaps. 28–30).
The cities of refuge (35:9–34).

New Laws

Other sections deal with entirely new provisions, such as:

The law of jealousy (5:11–28), which submits a wife to a test resembling an ordeal when a husband suspects her of unfaithfulness.
Regulations governing the vows of a Nazirite (6:1–21), meaning "one separated" (not "Nazarene"). Although all Israel is holy, these volunteer Nazirite vows demonstrate extraordinary consecration to God.
The cleansing of the Levites (8:5–26), who, like the priests, were admitted to their appointed service in the tabernacle only after the proper rite of installation.
Tassels (with one blue thread) on the garment corners (15:37–41) were to help a person "remember all the commandments of the LORD."
Purification through the ashes of a sacrificial red heifer (chap. 19), mixed in water with the ashes of cedar, hyssop, and scarlet, would cleanse a person defiled by contact with a corpse (5:2; 9:6).
Laws of inheritance (27:1–11; cf. 36:1–12) provide that a man without sons could pass his inheritance also through his daughters, provided that they married men of their own tribe.
The offerings for the seven days of Unleavened Bread (28:17–25).

LAWS TEMPORARY AND PERMANENT

Some of the laws and provisions are designed only for the period of desert wandering—for example, the grouping of the tribes about the tabernacle, the marching formations, the signals for beginning and ending a journey, and exclusion from the camp for various reasons.

Other laws were to apply at once and to remain in force ever afterward—for example, blowing the trumpets "for directing the movement of camps" on their journey (10:2), in war, and in celebration of appointed feasts and the regulations regarding the consecration and function of priests and Levites.

Many prescriptions deal only with the conquest and possession of Canaan—for example, driving out all the inhabitants of Canaan (33:50–56); marking the boundaries of the land (chap. 34); assigning 48 cities to the Levites (chap. 35), six as cities of refuge in the case of manslaughter.

Finally, some rites were to begin "when you have come into the land" (15:2)—for example, meal offerings (impossible in the desert) were to accompany the animal sacrifices (chaps. 15; 28; 29).

LAWS IN A FRAMEWORK OF EVENTS

Like Exodus and Leviticus, Numbers does not codify laws according to subject matter. But some legislative material and some new directives are added as certain situations develop.

The rights and duties of the Levites are enumerated in connection with their location within the camp, the formation of which required the taking of the census (chap. 1–4).

Further clarification of the authority of the Levites resulted from the uprising of the Levite Korah (16:1–7).

The allotment of 48 cities to the Levites (chap. 35) follows the provisions for dividing "the land among you as an inheritance" (34:16–29).

The Levites' purification for service appears in the context of the completion of the tabernacle (chap. 8; cf. 7:1).

The law regarding female inheritance (27:1–11; 36) grew out of the second census, during which a man named Zelophehad was found to have only daughters (26:33).

After the defeat of the Midianites, rules for the conduct of war became necessary (31:14–31).

Such obvious connections do not always exist. For example,

although laws regarding the removal of unclean persons from the camp (5:1–4) follow the setting up of the camp (chaps. 1–4), the immediately following statutes (i.e., regarding restitution for wrong, the law of jealousy, and the prescription for a Nazirite; 5:5–6:21) have no direct connection with the camp itself.

Particularly after their arrival in the plains of Moab (22:1), legislation tends to anticipate the future (e.g., chaps. 28–29, concerning offerings in the land, mentioned after Moses' successor is named in 27:12–23).

The explicit reference to future sacrifices "when you come into the land of Canaan" (34:1) appears to support the conclusion of some scholars that sacrifices were suspended for the 38 years after Israel's exclusion from Canaan. Other factors also favor this view. For example, Scripture makes no reference to the performance of sacrifices nor to the setting up of the tabernacle during these 38 years. Even such a basic ceremony as circumcision was neglected (Joshua 5:5–8). Centuries later, the prophet Amos asks (expecting a negative reply), "Did you offer Me sacrifices and offerings in the wilderness forty years, O house of Israel?" (Amos 5:25; later quoted by Stephen, Acts 7:42).

• • • • •

"The Lord Bless You"

Though the value of the book of Numbers remains much the same as for Leviticus, the new covenant reader finds embedded in this book a special blessing that his or her own appointed "Aaron" pronounces in worship: the so-called Aaronic blessing (6:24–26):

> *The Lord bless you and keep you;*
> *The Lord make His face shine upon you,*
> *And be gracious to you;*
> *The Lord lift up His countenance upon you,*
> *And give you peace.*

Here, if nowhere else in the book, the old and new covenants meet. Old Testament Israel and its spiritual descendants have the same history of salvation and the same giver of blessing, grace, and peace. Both are numbered in God's heavenly "Book of Numbers" because the Mediator between God and humanity "was numbered with the transgressors" (Mark 15:28; Is. 53:12)— transgressors of both covenants. No one is a mere number, a statistical digit to be added into a total. Each is a "you" (singular), who is blessed and kept in peace.

7. Deuteronomy

Deuteronomy continues where Numbers leaves off. The setting and time remain the same: the Plains of Moab east of the Jordan in the 40th and final year of the Exodus.[1] The two books also share an immediate and explicit concern for the people and the covenant "when you come into the land of Canaan" (Num. 34:2).

But in Deuteronomy a greater urgency dominates its message. The long-awaited thing is about to happen, and the people must prepare for it. They must remember their past and commit themselves to the future under God's gracious covenant.

THE SETTING WITHIN COVENANT HISTORY

In most of Deuteronomy events of the past (often in story form) are interwoven into the fabric of Moses' long discourses about the covenant and its laws. Deuteronomy differs from Numbers in the way it relates history to legislation. In Numbers, instruction was given as historical situations arose. In Deuteronomy, history becomes a part of the instruction itself as Moses underscores God's presence and activity in all the events that brought Israel to that time and place (events for the most part already recorded in Exodus through Numbers[2]).

This use of history to elucidate and emphasize the key elements of the covenant becomes more meaningful when one considers the circumstances and the concerns of Moses.

Previously, the people had in their midst the mediator of the covenant, but they had not often listened to him. Moses therefore makes one final grand plea for faithfulness to the covenant obligations.

Knowing that he is about to die, Moses is concerned that Israel follow his successor as God's appointed one.

---

[1]Verse 1 seems to indicate that Moses delivered the substance of these addresses when Israel first arrived at Kadesh two years after leaving Egypt. When they returned to Kadesh 38 years later, the new situation demanded that the same directions be given again.

[2]In some instances Deuteronomy adds a new feature or detail not previously included. E.g., in Num. 13:1–2 the spies were sent by Moses at God's command. Deut. 1:22–23 adds that Israel originally had requested this precautionary measure. Additional examples can readily be found.

An entirely new generation faced Moses. Not one (save Joshua and Caleb) of the original "signers" of the covenant at Sinai was present. This was a new people. They could shrug off all responsibility and say, "Our fathers may have said, 'All that the Lord says, we will do,' but *we* have made no such promise." Does this new generation that stands before him truly believe that the covenant made at Sinai was made with and for them and was not just a thing of the past?

If so, do they understand with their heart, soul, and mind the implications of obedient commitment?

Furthermore, Israel had arrived just recently in the Plains of Moab; yet two-and-a-half tribes already were situated in their permanent lands. Would they renege on helping the other tribes?

When the people have taken possession of the land and have begun to enjoy its fruits, will they still feel a need for the Lord? Or will they be tempted to say, "The covenant was made in the desert for the desert; it does not apply to life in Canaan"?

Since Israel had "played the harlot" at its first contact with idolatrous practice in Moab (Num. 25), what would the people do when they would encounter it at every turn in Canaan? Would Israel actually exterminate the idolatrous people of Canaan and their places of worship?

These concerns shape the discourses in Deuteronomy and reveal the urgency in what Moses has to say "today" (4:40, et al.) if in the days in Canaan the covenant is not to become extinct.

General Overview

DEUTERONOMY: CONTINUATION OF THE LAW

Deuteronomy ("repetition" or "second giving of the Law") represents the last cycle of covenant instruction. Clearly centered in the Decalog, this final concentric circle of legislation supplements and occasionally modifies previous laws. Two examples illustrate the relationship of Deuteronomy to previous legislation as well as its deliberate adaption of known laws to changing conditions.[3]

In 16:1–12 the directions for the celebration of the Passover

---

[3]Deuteronomy also includes sections of legislation applicable only to settled life in Canaan—e.g., concerning false and true prophets (13:1–11; 18:20–22), concerning the kingship (17:14–20), and concerning the conduct of war (chap. 20).

assume an acquaintance with earlier instructions for it (e.g., Ex. 12:1–20) and repeat only some of the provisions. But Deuteronomy adapts one point: As long as Israel was encamped at the tabernacle in the wilderness, this festival was to be observed within each household. But after the conquest, Israel was to leave its households (Deut. 16:5) and still gather "at the place where the LORD your God chooses to make His name abide" (v. 6). In Canaan, attendance at the central sanctuary would require the worshipers to assemble there no matter how far from their homes.

As the second example, note that during the journey all animals that were to be eaten had to be slaughtered at the door of the tabernacle (Lev. 17) except when anyone "catches any animal or bird that may be eaten" (v. 13). Such a requirement would be unrealistic and punitive in Canaan. Therefore, "when the LORD your God enlarges your border, . . . and you say, 'Let me eat meat,' . . . you may eat as much meat as your heart desires. If the place where the LORD your God chooses to put His name is too far from you, then you may slaughter from your herd and from your flock, . . . and you may eat within your gates" (Deut. 12:20–22).

MOSES' THREE SERMONS

In Deuteronomy, Moses the lawgiver and historian shows himself to be a preacher and orator of the first magnitude as he uses a rhetorical, admonitory style. His three main discourses are:

1:6–4:40

Moses' opening address delivers a general call to obedience in remembrance of God's gracious dealings with Israel in the past.

4:44–28:68

This long section exhorts Israel to covenant faithfulness. Chapters 4–11 treat the continuing validity of the covenant and its demand for a total response to the God who established it. Chapters 12–26 review the special judgments and statutes according to which the covenant nation is to regulate its social, ethical, economic, and religious life in Canaan. Chapters 27–28 reinforce the ongoing authority of Moses' word by instructing the people to inscribe the Law on large stones at Mount Ebal, just across the Jordan. As unchangeable as words engraved on stone, so unalterably sure are the curses for disobedience and the blessings for obedience that Israel could expect.

29:1–30:20

Moses reminds the people that they now have the opportunity to "enter into the covenant of the LORD" fully trusting in His continued favor, but they should do so also in full realization that they are confronting a decision of "life and good, death and evil" (30:15).

HISTORICAL EVENTS IN DEUTERONOMY

Although most of the events in Deuteronomy are remembered history as retold by Moses, some action does take place.

The setting is "on this side of the Jordan . . . in the fortieth year, in the eleventh month, on the first day of the month" (1:1, 3).

Three cities of refuge were established on the eastern side of the Jordan, one in each of the tribal lands allotted to Reuben, Gad, and the half-tribe of Manasseh (4:41–43).

Chapters 31–34 include a few brief notes about Moses' activity in anticipation of his death, *activity motivated and controlled by his concern for Israel's future as the covenant people.* In response to the Lord's direction, Moses . . .

wrote the law of the covenant in a book (31:9) and had it placed beside the Ark of the Covenant (31:24–26) as a reminder to read it regularly and at specified times (31:10–13);

presented himself and Joshua in the tent of meeting (31:14–15) for the latter's commissioning (v. 23) as the leader who would conquer Canaan as promised in the covenant;

composed a song inculcating covenant history and principles and warning against unfaithfulness to it (31:19, 30–32:43);

had Joshua join him in teaching the song to Israel (31:19; 32:44);

blessed the 12 tribes as Jacob had once blessed his 12 sons before departing this life (chap. 33; cf. Gen. 48:1–49:28);

ascended Mount Nebo and was granted a view of all the land of Canaan, which he was forbidden to enter (32:48–52; 34:1–4; cf. Num. 20:1–13); and

"died there in the land of Moab, according to the word of the LORD. . . . And the children of Israel wept for Moses in the plains of Moab thirty days" (34:5, 8).

Moses' Covenant Teaching

OVERVIEW

Moses' great concern in the Plains of Moab was that the covenant not become a thing of the past.

The introduction to his discourses reflects his desire to make a lasting impression on his hearers: "Moses began to explain this law" (1:5). The Hebrew word for explain actually means "to engrave" and is used only here as "explain." Moses wanted to *inscribe*—indelibly write—this law on the hearts of his people; for the time was coming soon when he would no longer be alive to repeat it himself. Moses therefore provided for the law to be engraved[4] on stone (27:1–8) soon after his death "when you cross over the Jordan."

Moses put all his powers of persuasion and oratory into applying the law to his listeners. He appealed; he illustrated; he pleaded; he threatened; he summarized; he itemized; he repeated. His words are charged with a sense of crisis and finality. They reflect the warm compassion in the heart of a man whose life since the burning bush had been devoted to his people. He shows urgent concern for the future based on years of experience with a fickle people.

Second, he worked to persuade the present generation of Israelites, old and young, to become part of God's plan, to "enter into covenant with the LORD your God, and into His oath, which the LORD your God makes with you today" (29:12). In 28 chapters he explains the past, present, and future significance of the covenant. Only then (in chap. 29) does he expect Israel to act on the basis of his instruction and to enter into the covenant as did their fathers.

Moses taught well. Certain lessons are repeated again and again, as if to engrave them. Yet they all have one major objective: to enable the Israelites to see themselves in the perspective of the unchanging covenant of the unchanging God. The outcome was to be a whole-souled participation.

FOCI IN MOSES' MESSAGE

Although each of the three discourses has its own emphasis, the basic points weave back and forth between them, providing a continuous, unified whole.

---

[4]The same Hebrew word for "explain" is used here as in 1:5. The word occurs once elsewhere of writing on stone: in Hab. 2:2 where two verses later the famous words to be inscribed include "the just shall live by his faith."

1. The Covenant Land As "Promised Land"

The opening words of the first sermon stress Israel's conquest of Canaan as part of a long-range plan of God.

> See, I have set the land before you; go in and possess the land which the LORD swore to your fathers—to Abraham, Isaac, and Jacob—to give to them and their descendants after them. (1:8)[5]

The conquest of Canaan would not be a national achievement or the result of natural cause and effect. Without the promise to the fathers there would be no conquest. The Promised Land was to be theirs only as heirs of the promise.

2. Continuing Validity of the Covenant

Moses recalled many events of the past to show how God had been fulfilling this promise ever since the Exodus began. But most often he called attention to the history of the past few months: the defeat of the Amorite kings, Og and Sihon, the most recent link in the chain of events that firmly bound this people to the covenant made with the patriarchs. Moses' purpose seems obvious—everyone in his audience had experienced the event. Though many had been born after other victories, no one could say of this one, "I don't know whether your story is true." This victory over the Amorites proved to all, young and old, that they had overcome not by their own strength but by God's. Possession of the land would be possible only because "I give it to you."

Moses also had to impress on his listeners in sharp and precise language the contemporary nature and continuing validity of the covenant. Therefore, he said to people who were but children or not even born yet at the time of Sinai,

> The LORD our God made a covenant with *us* in Horeb. The LORD did not make this covenant with our fathers, but with us, those who are here today, all of us who are alive. The LORD talked with *you* face to face on the mountain from the midst of the fire. (5:2–4, emphasis added)

With an eye toward asking this new people to commit itself to the covenant, Moses emphasized that thereby they would enter into a relationship with God *identical* to what He had established with their fathers at Horeb (Mount Sinai). The presuppositions, terms, and obligations of the covenant had not changed after 40 years—and they were to remain unchanged. To be the covenant people, Israel is required always

---

[5]Moses recalls this oath to the fathers about 25 times in Deuteronomy.

> to fear the LORD your God, to walk in all His ways and to love Him, to serve the LORD your God with all your heart and with all your soul, and to keep the commandments of the LORD and His statutes. (10:12–13)

The basis and foundation of instruction in God's will were laid down once and for all in the Ten Commandments engraved on two tables of stone (4:13). Now Moses engraves them on his hearers' hearts by repeating them verbatim (5:6–21)[6] before using them as the text of an extended sermon (5:22–11:32). Israel's covenant status depends on continued obedience to these basic and all-embracing requirements of undivided loyalty to God.

3. Covenant Forms and Ceremonies

Furthermore, God had required at Sinai that the people observe outward forms and ceremonies. Moses proceeded to remind the living generation also of these covenant obligations to be

> a holy people to the LORD, your God . . . [chosen] to be a people for Himself, a special treasure above all the peoples who are on the face of the earth. (14:2; cf. 7:6)

The moral, cultic, social, and political expressions of their separation from all other nations and total consecration to God were designed not merely for the desert, but

> you shall be careful to observe [them] in the land which the LORD God of your fathers is giving you to possess, all the days that you live on the earth. (12:1)

Moses repeats many of these provisions in his second discourse (chaps. 12–26), fully expounding some and making minor adjustments in a few to meet the needs of life in the Promised Land.

4. The Covenant of God's Grace

Just as the Ten Commandments remained the same, so did the terms of the covenant shaping God's relationship to His people. The covenant would never be based on merit. It would remain His instrument of grace to a people that had not and never would deserve what He had bound and pledged Himself to give in the promises to the patriarchs and to the fathers at Sinai.

The covenant had to be of grace. From the beginning Israel

---

[6]Some scholars believe that the Decalog strictly speaking consisted only of the 10 brief words or sentences inscribed on the stone tables. Therefore, the slight differences between Ex. 20 and Deut. 5 result from Moses' divinely inspired interpretive comments appropriate to these two separate occasions.

stubbornly had broken the covenant often, shamefully, and defiantly. Moses reminds them:

> Remember and do not forget how you provoked the LORD your God to wrath in the wilderness; from the day that you departed from the land of Egypt until you came to this place, you have been rebellious against the LORD. (9:7)

5. Obedience and Repentance

In view of Israel's past performance, Moses rightly worried whether the people would or could continue as the covenant nation. If the people persist in breaking the covenant by their disobedience, God has no obligation to keep them as His covenant people. He even will deprive them again of the land they have not quite inherited.

On the other hand, the God who began the covenant with the patriarchs and the fathers at Sinai also promises to continue to show mercy to those who love Him and keep His commandments. As in the past, He will receive back into His grace those who penitently plead for His forgiving mercy. God's power has not grown weaker. He can and will bless beyond expectation, for

> indeed heaven and the highest heavens belong to the LORD your God, also the earth with all that is in it. The LORD delighted only in your fathers, to love them; and He chose their descendants after them, you above all peoples, as it is this day. (10:14–15)

6. Future Temptation to Break the Covenant: Ease in Canaan

Moses anticipated unprecedented occasions of temptations to break the covenant once Israel had crossed the Jordan and taken possession of the land. If a previous generation had been willing to surrender God for the easy life of Egypt (compared to the wilderness), will not this generation also quickly forget God once it enjoys what the Promised Land has to offer? Thus, Moses warns,

> Beware that you do not forget the LORD your God . . . when you have eaten and are full, and have built beautiful houses and dwell in them; and when your herds and your flocks multiply, and your silver and your gold are multiplied, and all that you have is multiplied; . . . [and] you say in your heart, "My power and the might of my hand have gained me this wealth." (8:11–13, 17)

7. Future Temptation to Break the Covenant: Idolatry

Similarly, Moses was apprehensive of Israel's future exposure to idolatry. If they had "played the harlot" at their first contact with idolatrous practice in Moab (Num. 25), what would they do when they encountered it at every turn in Canaan? God therefore directed the Israelites to exterminate the idolatrous people of Canaan and to destroy their places of worship, their altars, and all their paraphernalia for idolatry.

In this context the direction from God to set up an altar on Mount Ebal after the entry into Canaan takes on importance. This is one of 18 times in Deuteronomy in which God specifies that "you shall seek the place where the LORD your God chooses, out of all your tribes, to put His name for His dwelling place" (12:5).

In Canaanite idolatry, the gods could be manipulated to do the bidding of the people. Not so with the one God, Yahweh. He is not at the disposal of His worshipers wherever or whenever they desire to put Him into their service by magic and incantation. Nor is He a force of nature to be controlled. Since He is God the Almighty, *He* will choose the places of worship according to His good pleasure and according to the exigencies of developing circumstances.

Moses wanted Israel to enter the Promised Land forewarned and forearmed. To do so, they had to keep the first commandment above all: "You shall have no other gods before me." Moses explained this commandment and summed up its positive teaching in the great *Shema* (so-called for its opening Hebrew word):

Hear, O Israel:
The LORD our God, the LORD is one! (6:4)

Moses' Place in History

Moses' death marks the end of an epoch. There was never to arise again "in Israel a prophet like Moses, whom the LORD knew face to face" (34:10). By God's choice and grace, Moses was "the man of God" and "the servant of the LORD" (33:1; 34:5).

Moses mediated a covenant that endured for centuries, and then its outward forms ended. When *the* Prophet, the Word made flesh, arrived, what was preparatory in the old covenant for God's ultimate covenant was absorbed in fulfillment. As God's spokesman, Moses transmitted to and defined for Israel a way of life with God based on faith in the promise of His unearned, merciful forgiveness. "By it [faith] the men of old received divine approval" (Heb. 11:2 RSV), and it is still possible to be saved only by faith, by "looking unto Jesus, the author and finisher of our faith" (Heb. 12:2). Faith in God's forgiveness (the faith of both covenants) is valid for only one reason: the Lamb of God who took away the sins of the world.

The demand of the law (God's call for full outward and inward devotion to Him) also remains in force. It was fulfilled by Him who was put under the curse of the law (Gal. 3:10–13), but He did not destroy the law (Matt. 5:17–20). For He also requires, "If you love Me, keep My commandments" (John 14:15). No less demanding than the Mosaic law, His commandments are identical with the Old Testament summary of its law:

> "You shall love the LORD your God with all your heart, with all your soul, and with all your mind." This is the first and great commandment. And the second is like it: "You shall love your neighbor as yourself." On these two commandments hang all the Law and the Prophets. (Matt. 22:37–40; cf. Deut. 6:5; Lev. 19:18)

Therefore, Jesus could make the sweeping and unqualified statement, "Moses . . . wrote of Me" (John 5:46). Not a verse or chapter only, but all the words of this prophet point to Him and come to rest in Him.

On the road to Emmaus, when Jesus explained to the two disciples "in all the Scriptures the things concerning Himself" (Luke 24:27), He began with Moses.

• • • • •

Underneath Are the Everlasting Arms

The last recorded words of Moses are his blessing on the individual tribes of Israel (Deut. 33). Like many of the "judgments and statutes" that Moses presented, his parting words about tribal prosperity may leave modern readers untouched (except for some appreciation of its poetic imagery and language).

But as the Aaronic Blessing (Num. 6:24–26) draws today's readers into the circle of the old covenant, so do some of the closing words of Moses' blessing. God pronounces it on them too, for they share in the blessing on Israel of old. Together with Israel, believers of all ages bow their heads before the same God and receive the same assurance: "The eternal God is your refuge, and underneath are the everlasting arms" (33:27).

Moses' arms had grown weary in the battle with the Amalekites and soon now would be rigidly helpless in death. Yet he knew that the arms of God are always present with everlasting strength. They remain outstretched even when God says today as He did to Moses, "Return, O children of men" (Ps. 90:3).

God led Israel out of Egypt and into Canaan "with an outstretched arm" (Deut. 26:8) also for people today. For out of those tribes of the desert came He who put God's arms under all His people. Because He takes away the sins of the world, every believer can confidently repeat Jesus' dying words to God, "Father, 'into Your hands I commend My spirit' " (Luke 23:46).

8. Joshua

The book begins with the words "after the death of Moses," but covenant history does not depend even on the greatest and noblest of men. God provided (as He always does) a Joshua to succeed a Moses—fearful though the people might be of a future without him with whom God "spoke face to face."

In spite of human frailties and instability, God's dealings with His people as a whole often revolve around individuals who have become great because of their service to the God who chose them. Thus, this book bears the name of Moses' "understudy," and its contents constitute another chapter that ends as the next one begins (Judg. 1:1)—"after the death of Joshua."

Events in Joshua

Scripture does not provide enough detail to determine the length of this Joshua epoch. Two items are mentioned: (1) Joshua was 110 years old when he died (24:29), and (2) his parting addresses to the people shortly before his death took place "a long time after the LORD had given rest to Israel from all their enemies round about" (23:1). But Joshua's age when the book opens is not told. Thus one can only conjecture that the span may have been about 50 years, based on the assumption that Joshua was at least of "arms bearing age" (20) when he spied out the land (Ex. 33:11). That plus the 38 additional years in the wilderness would make him close to 60 years old when Moses died, and an additional 50 years would bring him to 110 at his death.

MILITARY CAMPAIGNS (CHAPTERS 1–12)

Establishing a Beachhead (Chapters 1–9)

After crossing the Jordan (chaps. 1–4), the Israelites experienced no initial opposition as they celebrated the Passover (and reinstituted circumcision, chap. 5), for the Canaanite kings' "heart[s] melted; and there was no spirit in them any longer" when they "heard that the LORD had dried up the waters of the Jordan" (5:1).

The Israelites having recommitted themselves to the Lord, Joshua began to establish a beachhead in the central hill country.

To do so, he[1] first destroyed Jericho at the line between the hills to the west and the Jordan valley to the east. Israel then moved into the hills themselves to destroy the city of Ai (near another of God's holy places, Bethel). In each case, the miraculous and direct intervention of God is stressed, particularly in the case of Ai.

Israel first attacked after spying out the city, concluding that weak Ai could be taken without God's intervention. Although that would have been humanly possible, Israel was badly defeated because a man named Achan had secretly and disobediently kept for himself spoils from the fall of Jericho. Only after the sin was uncovered and Israel had showed its repentance in the execution of Achan did God give Ai into the hand of Joshua (chaps. 7–8).

At Shechem[2] in the valley between Mount Ebal and Mount Gerizim, Joshua built an altar at the direction of God through Moses (Deut. 27:4–5) and sacrificed on it, inscribed "a copy of the law of Moses," and read to the people "all the words of the law, . . . all that Moses had commanded" (Joshua 8:30–35).

As part of God's constant emphasis on following His direction for taking the land, chapter 9 relates how Gibeon, a city a little south of Ai, escaped destruction and remained in the land as a continual temptation to idolatry. Using a ruse, the Gibeonites convinced the leaders of Israel to pledge not to harm this city, supposedly so far away that "all the bread of their provision was dry and moldy" by the time they arrived at Israel's camp. When the trick was discovered too late, Israel still kept its pledge to Gibeon because "we have sworn to them by the Lord God of Israel." But Israel did make them their servants in the land.

Expansion Southward (Chapter 10)

The first major attempt to dislodge Israel from its position in central Canaan involved five kings south of the occupied territory, headed by the king of Jerusalem immediately to the south. They had heard that Jericho and Ai, acting individually, had been destroyed. (They were angry that Gibeon, also working individually, had bargained with Israel for its safety.) The five kings felt that their only hope was a united defense and a joint counterattack.

---

[1]In spite of references to Joshua's actions, all victories in the book are credited to Yahweh: "See! I have given Jericho into your hand" (6:2)—and that before the battle had begun.

[2]God had long established Shechem as a holy place where He would communicate with His chosen ones. Abraham, after having been called out of Haran, received God's reiteration of the promise at Shechem (Gen. 12:6–7). After Jacob arrived safely back in Canaan with his wives and children, he built an altar at Shechem. Here Joshua buried the bones of Joseph, which the Israelites had brought from Egypt (Joshua 24:32).

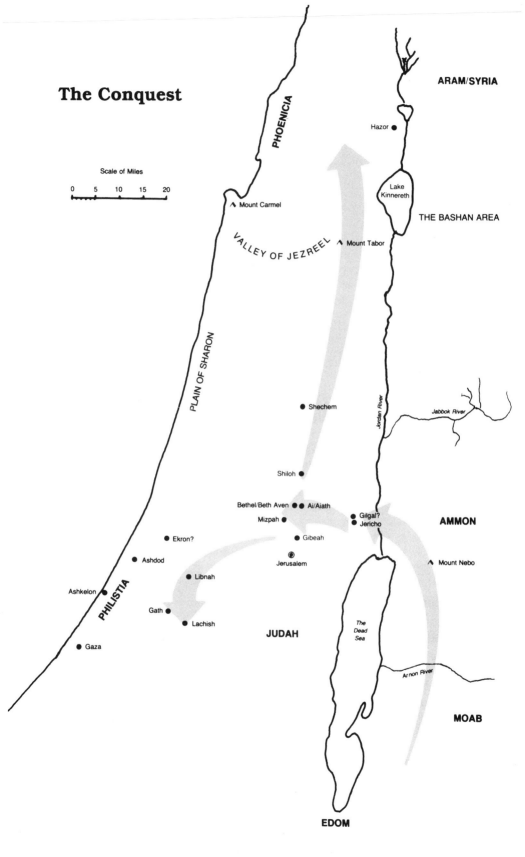

The Conquest

ARAM/SYRIA

PHOENICIA

Hazor ●

Scale of Miles

0   5   10   15   20

∧ Mount Carmel

Lake
Kinnereth

THE BASHAN AREA

VALLEY OF JEZREEL   ∧ Mount Tabor

PLAIN OF SHARON

Jordan River

Jabbok River

● Shechem

Shiloh ●

Bethel/Beth Aven ● ● Ai/Aiath

Mizpah ●

● Gilgal?
● Jericho

AMMON

Ekron? ●

● Gibeah

Ashdod ●

◎
Jerusalem

∧ Mount Nebo

Ashkelon ●

PHILISTIA

● Libnah

Gath ●

● Lachish

JUDAH

The
Dead
Sea

● Gaza

Arnon River

MOAB

EDOM

Their strategy was to attack Gibeon, thus baiting Israel to come to the aid of its new ally.

That happened, but Joshua defeated their combined forces and carried the war into their home territory as far south as Kadesh-Barnea. The five kings didn't have a chance, for "the LORD routed them before Israel . . . because the LORD God of Israel fought for Israel" (10:10, 42). The Lord even provided extra time for this victory by making the sun stand still (verses 12–14).

Expansion Northward and Recapitulation (Chapters 11–12)

From the north a second coalition of Canaanites threatened Israel (11:1–15). Its leader was the king of Hazor, north of the Sea of Galilee, "by the waters of Merom" (v. 7). In this case Joshua did not wait for the attack but took the offensive.

The brief report of Joshua's campaign does not explain how Joshua was able to pass through hitherto unconquered territory guarded by such formidable fortresses as Migiddo and Taanach (12:21).

What is told (though in barest terms) is that Hazor's joint forces had every advantage, including chariots. Yet these also vanished before Joshua because "the LORD delivered them into the hand of Israel" (11:8). From Hazor Joshua pursued them as far north as Greater Sidon. "So all the cities of those kings, and all their kings, Joshua took and struck with the edge of the sword. He utterly destroyed them. . . . But as for the cities, . . . Israel burned none of them, except Hazor only" (vv. 12–13).

Chapter 12 tabulates the victories of Israel over the Canaanites on both sides of the Jordan.

> So Joshua took the whole land, according to all that the LORD had said to Moses; and Joshua gave it as an inheritance to Israel according to their divisions by their tribes. Then the land rested from war. (v. 23)

Comments on the Conquest

To understand this history, a number of basic factors in the account must be placed into clear perspective.

First, these chapters provide a summary record. Other battles with the Canaanites took place in addition to those briefly described here (cf. the list of 31 defeated kings in 12:7–24). "Joshua made war a long time with all those kings" (11:18).

Second, when more is added beyond a mere mention of names, the detail demonstrates that without the miraculous intervention of God, Israel could not have won a victory (much less have ever set foot into Canaan). What was impossible became easy when the Lord gave victory; what seemed easy (like attacking Ai) became impossible without Him.

Third, Joshua's achievements must not be exaggerated beyond what the account expressly states. (1) He directed the joint effort of all the tribes, but (2) that joint effort had a limited goal. It is that limited goal to which we turn our attention.

That it was a joint effort can be seen in the attention called to the two and a half tribes east of the Jordan who participated in the campaigns west of the Jordan and their dismissal by Joshua at the end of these battles. This joint effort contrasts strongly with the later attempts by individual tribes to take possession of their assigned territories.

But Joshua's assignment was not to lead Israel until it occupied all of Canaan, not even until it had occupied the territories where God's people had achieved military victory. The record clearly distinguished between victory in battle and the permanent settlement of Israel.

Joshua sought to (and did) eliminate the most imminent threat to Israel's foothold in Canaan, and he did this as the leader of a military supplied by a united people. When he finished this task, the back of Canaanite power was broken, and so "the land rested from war" (11:23).

During this period of rest, Joshua carried out God's second objective: allotting the land. Note that Joshua supervised only the allotment; he did not direct a unified endeavor to possess the land on behalf of the individual tribes.

The fourth basic factor to keep in perspective is the distinction between taking the land in battle and occupying or possessing it. If the difference is obscured, the book of Joshua may seem to make little sense. With careful reading, one can detect this nuance in chapter 12. This summary of events begins by listing "the kings of the land whom the children of Israel *defeated*, and whose land they *possessed*" east of the Jordan under Moses' leadership (v. 1, emphasis added). The second part of the chapter lists "the kings of the country which Joshua and the children of Israel *conquered* on this [west] side of the Jordan, . . . *which Joshua gave* to the tribes of Israel *as a possession* according to their divisions" (v. 7, emphasis added). The verb "possessed" (or "take possession") is conspicuously absent in connection with Joshua's activity with the people as a whole. True, Joshua gave certain areas of Canaan "as a possession," but in this modifying clause, the connotation is of giving the territory "to be a possession."[3]

---

[3]NKJV: "So the LORD gave to Israel all the land, . . . and they took possession

God's marching orders to Joshua had not included the occupation of the land. The people were to "cross over this Jordan, to go in to possess the land which the LORD your God is giving you to possess" (1:11), but nothing is said of Joshua's leadership in attaining this ultimate goal. Joshua's work is restricted to a "softening up" operation against the enemy. This limitation is made explicit in the account of the allotment of the land (chaps. 13–21, particularly 13:1). There God reminds Joshua of his advanced age and of the big task he leaves unfinished. "There remains very much land yet to be *possessed*" (emphasis added). Then follows a list of the areas that remain, that were unpossessed at this juncture, and the promise of God, "I will drive [them] out from before the children of Israel; only divide it by lot to Israel as an inheritance" (13:1–6). Acting on pure faith, therefore, Joshua was to divide the land and give it as an inheritance *before* it was conquered or possessed. (Although the land was allotted, the next step, the full occupation of the land, was thwarted by Israel's lassitude and weak faith—as reported later.)

ALLOTTING THE LAND (CHAPTERS 13–22)

The allotment of the land was achieved in five stages.

1. Moses earlier had allotted the territory east of the Jordan to the tribes of Reuben and Gad and half the tribe of Manasseh (Joshua 13:8–32).
2. Probably at Gilgal (14:6), Joshua allotted territory to Judah (15:1–12, 20–63).
3. Ephraim and the other half of Manasseh receive their allotment (16:1–17:18), perhaps also at Gilgal.[4]
4. Since the tribe of Levi was not to receive a special territory but cities within the lands of other tribes, only seven tribes remained to receive an allotment. This happened at Shiloh (18:1), where Joshua allotted land to the tribes of Benjamin, Simeon, Zebulun, Issachar, Asher, Naphtali, and Dan (18:1–19:4).
5. Finally came the allotment of cities of refuge (chap. 20) and of the cities of the tribe of Levi (chap. 21). The latter were to be given place and supported by the whole nation

---

of it and dwelt in it." But compare TEV: "So the LORD gave to Israel all the land that he had solemnly promised their ancestors. . . . When they had taken possession of it, they settled down there" (21:43).

[4]Four tribes but really five groups (Reuben, Gad, Judah, and Joseph's two sons, Manasseh and Ephraim; cf. Gen. 48:5–6) have been allotted. Jacob's 13th child, daughter Dinah, did not receive a land inheritance.

The Division

Asher

Naphtali

Zebulun

Issachar

Manasseh

Ephraim

Gad

Benjamin

Dan

Jerusalem

Reuben

Judah

Simeon

in recognition of their services to all the tribes. The priests, the descendants of Aaron, were to receive 13 cities in the vicinity of Jerusalem (21:4); the rest of the Levites were scattered among the other tribal possessions on both sides of the Jordan.

The book of Joshua does not say that the tribes actually occupied the lands that were allotted to them. The author of Judges explicitly states that it was "after the death of Joshua" (Judg. 1:1) and "when Joshua had dismissed the . . . children of Israel" (2:6) that the people began to possess the land. Judges also provides the reasons why some tribes were unable actually to occupy and settle in their patrimony as Joshua had defined it.

As a postscript to the military campaigns, Joshua blessed the armed forces of the two and a half tribes from east of the Jordan who had faithfully contributed their part to these battles and sent them on their way (chap. 22). "The LORD your God has given rest to your brethren; . . . now therefore, return and go to your tents" (v. 4). Divided by the Jordan from their brothers, the eastern tribes expressed their solidarity with those on the west side by building an altar at the Jordan (vv. 10, 24–29, 34).

JOSHUA'S PARTING WORDS (CHAPTERS 23–24)

Joshua's mission was accomplished. He was old and well advanced in years. As to the possession of the land, God would dispossess the nations that remained after Joshua's death if the tribes "keep and . . . do all that is written in the Book of the Law of Moses" (23:6). But "God will no longer drive out these nations" if the Israelites "go back, and cling to the remnant of these nations—these that remain among" them (vv. 12–13).

Therefore, Joshua's final act was to induce Israel to commit and pledge itself to the covenant (24:1–15). Like Moses, he reminded the tribes at Shechem of God's undeserved grace from the days of Abraham to the entry into the Promised Land. The people acknowledged that the fear of the Lord drove out (not "dispossessed") before them all the Canaanites, and that the unfinished business of occupying their inheritance would be completed only if they remained faithful to the Lord and join with Joshua in saying, "As for me and my house, we will serve the LORD" (v. 15).

The book closes with a brief mention of Joshua's death (v. 29) and that of Eleazar, the high priest, son of Aaron (v. 33).

The Book of Joshua and the Covenant

Joshua, a "Second Moses"

Joshua's career parallels that of Moses in several ways. Perhaps the most striking similarity occurred when the "Commander of the army of the LORD" encountered Joshua and commanded him to "take your sandal off your foot, for the place where you stand is holy" (5:13–15; cf. Ex. 3:5).

Other similarities include God's promise to be with Joshua as He was with Moses (1:5), the people's promise of loyalty (1:16–18—though Moses often had to deal with their rebelliousness and unfaithfulness), the miraculous crossing of the Jordan River on dry land (3:14–17), reinstituting the Passover and the rite of circumcision (5:2–10), the writing of the Law on tables of stone (8:32), and reestablishing the covenant (24:1–25).

But Joshua's leadership of Israel also differed from that of Moses in two ways. First, no lapse from faith is recorded of Joshua as it is of Moses (but less of Joshua's personal history is given than of Moses'). Second, although Moses had to cope with a rebellious people at every turn, no general revolt against Joshua is mentioned. In fact, the book's closing notes that "Israel served the LORD all the days of Joshua, and all the days of the elders who outlived Joshua, who had known all the works of the LORD which He had done for Israel" (24:31).

Yet the author of this book, by including particularly those events similar to the life of Moses, stressed the continuity of Israel's history under the undeviating purpose of God.

Focus on the Covenant

The covenant with the patriarchs and with Israel at Sinai is the axiomatic presupposition, the central, controlling factor of everything recorded in Joshua. And the book emphasizes that the covenant includes "terms"—requirements on the part of God as well as of Israel.

> Through Israel God would fulfill His part of the covenant, His promise to carry out His plan of salvation for all the nations of the earth.
> Israel must be faithful as the covenant nation; its history depends on it. The book of Joshua makes crystal clear that Israel succeeds or fails in the measure that it remains God's instrument of the covenant. In every age God blesses those whom He chooses, and He curses those who defy Him. This simple formula solves the great question of history that otherwise remains in spite of every expla-

nation of human cause and effect. Without the covenant, history remains a mystery wrapped in a riddle.

As the book of Joshua bears witness, human beings are unable to produce this salvation-bringing history, this *Heilsgeschichte*. Only Yahweh can effect the miraculous defeat of the Canaanites as He directs the course of history for His purpose.

The correlation between history and the covenant did not begin either with Moses or at the time of Joshua. God had decreed the future to be *Heilsgeschichte* from the beginning, from the promise to Adam and Eve (Gen. 3:15)—and even before the foundation of the world (Eph. 1:4). The book of Joshua merely presents another act in the drama of salvation. Since the redemption of the world by the blood of the new covenant was God's ultimate purpose, every chapter of the old covenant is God's footprint in His undeviating, sovereign, and merciful march to Calvary.

The book of Joshua marks a significant milestone in covenant history: "Not a word failed of any good thing which the LORD had spoken to the house of Israel. All came to pass" (Joshua 21:45).[5] God solidly built His way of salvation on the roadbed of historical achievement, emphasizes the author. Events happen only in accordance with the fixed and unalterable principles of the Maker of the covenant and covenant history.

Therefore, covenant history does not develop artificially or magically. Blessings do not fall mechanically and ready-made into Israel's lap. Israel must labor to make them come true, and proper was the admonition to "be strong and of good courage" (1:6, 9).

Successes and Failures Under the Covenant

After God had graciously formed Jacob's descendants into His covenant people and named them as His own, He provided them a choice for the future: "If you will . . . then I will . . ." Joshua presented this either/or choice to the people at Shechem in the renewal of the covenant. They could continue on the path God established for them, or they could follow the road to destruction by rejecting the covenant.

Israel's success and failure are in direct proportion to covenant courage of faith and covenant obedience. God put His power over all the earth at Israel's disposal, but only as Israel tapped the resources of the Creator by accepting the covenant and its re-

---

[5]See Ex. 2:24 for a similar previous milestone.

sponsibilities could Israel overcome all odds. This axiom enables the reader to understand the terse statements of what Israel achieved and what it failed to accomplish in taking possession of Canaan. "By faith they passed through the Red Sea as by dry land. . . . By faith the walls of Jericho fell down" (Heb. 11:29–30). Walls crumbled and armies were routed when Israel armed itself with faith in the God of the covenant. Conversely, in the absence of the obedience of faith when and because "Israel has sinned, and they have also transgressed My covenant" (Joshua 7:11), Israel suffered defeat. In the defeat at Ai[6] (as previously mentioned), Israel's natural resources and strength could have been sufficient to overwhelm the enemy (v. 3). God therefore made it clear that without covenant faith resulting in obedience there would be no covenant victory.

Even after the death of Joshua, the strength or impotence of Israel always remained in strict proportion to the faithfulness of the tribes to the covenant. None of the tribes could occupy its allotted territory without divine aid.

Some tribes did let God fight for them. Listen to Caleb, for example: "It may be that the LORD will be with me, and I shall be able to drive them out as the LORD said" (14:12). On the other hand, "as for the Jebusites, the inhabitants of Jerusalem, the children of Judah could not them drive out" (15:63). The Ephramites "did not drive out the Canaanites who dwelt in Gezer" (16:10). "The children of Manasseh could not drive out the inhabitants of those cities" (e.g., Beth-shean, Taanach, Megiddo—17:12). Perhaps Joshua foresaw this, for already at the time of the allotment he rebuked the people: "How long will you neglect to go and possess the land which the LORD God of your Fathers has given you?" (18:3).

God's miraculous help was needed because some of the odds or circumstances that the tribes faced were overwhelming by human standards. Judah, for example, was no match for the people of the plains and their chariots of iron (Judg. 1:19). But the true problem was lack of confidence in God's help or the courage of faith to attempt the impossible. Iron chariots were nothing against the power of God in Joshua's obedience to the covenant (Joshua 11:6, 9; cf. Deut. 20:1). Nor were they a problem later when "the LORD routed Sisera and all his chariots and all his army with the edge of the sword before Barak" (Judg. 4:15). Similarly,

---

[6]The defeat itself does not negate God's seeming guarantee that no matter what, "no man shall be able to stand before you [Joshua] all the days of your life" (1:5). All God's promises are in the framework of the covenant, and without the covenant there is no promise.

if by faith the walls of Jericho fell, there was no fortress in Canaan that could have withstood the trumpet blasts of Israel's faith.

All the while, God was channelling this miraculous help through circumstances that outwardly appeared to follow a natural pattern of cause and effect. A wind or landslide dammed up the Jordan (3:13–16; cf. Ex. 14:21), and hailstones helped defeat the army of the coalition of five kings headed by Jerusalem (10:11). A naturalistic philosophy of history would say that these phenomena happened at an auspicious time, that Israel "got the breaks." But the faithful are able to see God's hand at work and sing,

> He [God] turned the sea into dry land;
> They went through the river on foot.
> There we will rejoice in Him.
> He rules by His power forever. (Ps. 66:6–7)

Therefore, the question of taking possession of the land was one of faith, not physical circumstances.

All this underscores that covenant history is real history in the sense that it did not take place in a vacuum. It was a protracted campaign of conquests and occupations (cf. Deut. 8:17–26). Everything was quite natural, and only the eye of faith could see God's power—as later Elisha and his young servant, surrounded by the Syrian army, saw that "the mountain was full of [God's] horses and chariots of fire" (2 Kings 6:17). When Israel marched with the courage of faith in obedience to the covenant, this unseen cavalry swept all opposition before them. When Israel did not, the Canaanite chariots of mere iron drove them back.

THE MORALITY OF WAR AND THE COVENANT

As one of the covenant stipulations, God required that Israel annihilate the Canaanites and all the inhabitants of the land, and all booty of war was to be destroyed or dedicated to the Lord.

> When the LORD, your God . . . delivers them over to you, you shall conquer them and utterly destroy them. You shall make no covenant with them nor show mercy to them. . . .
>
> Of the cities of these peoples which the LORD your God gives you as an inheritance, you shall let nothing that breathes remain alive. (Deut. 7:1–5; 20:16)

Israel obeyed (usually). "They utterly destroyed all that was in the city, both man and woman, young and old, ox and sheep and donkey, with the edge of the sword" (Joshua 6:21).

Some who read Joshua have claimed that this reflects a low standard of morality on the part of Israel, that Israel's morals and conception of God had not moved beyond a low level of development—and that this God of bloody savagery has nothing in common with the loving Father of the forgiving Jesus, who directed God's people to "love your enemies, bless those who curse you, do good to those who hate you, and pray for those who spitefully use you and persecute you" (Matt. 5:44).

But this charge rests on a subjective misconception about God that forgets that the God of love also is the God who sends wrath on all workers of iniquity. Without His wrath, His love is reduced to impotence and sentimentality. Without His wrath, there would have been no cleansing flood at the time of Noah, no purging of the land of Sodom and Gomorrah, and ultimately no need for His Son to take on Himself the Father's wrath for the sins of the whole world.

Behind this charge against the picture of God in Joshua lies the more difficult yet real question of evil in the world. How can God idly stand by while nations war against nations, while the destructive forces of nature devastate more cities than Israel ever did, while individuals deliberately and premeditatively select innocent victims for torture, abuse, and murder? Although whole tomes have been written on this subject, it is treated but briefly here.

Jesus Himself did not address the problem directly. For example, He ignores the cause of the calamity at the tower of Siloam, but uses the occasion to call His disciples to repentance. But Jesus does give a clearer comment when His disciples asked about a handicapped man: " 'Who sinned, this man or his parents, that he was born blind?' Jesus answered, 'Neither this man nor his parents sinned, but that the works of God should be revealed in him' " (John 9:2–3).

The reader of Joshua (as well as most of the Old Testament) must keep in mind that God there provides *Heilsgeschichte*, a condensed history of His involvement with humanity to bring about the salvation of the world through the Seed to be born out of His covenant people, Israel. That goal of God cannot let sinful nations or peoples stand in the way—and that included the pagan peoples of Canaan who could lead Israel into idolatry (as actually happened because Israel did not obey God's command utterly to destroy them). On the other hand, God at times chose to use sinful nations to accomplish his purposes. For example, God chose Assyria and Babylon to be His agents of punishment against the northern and southern kingdoms and then chose a Persian, Cyrus, to be His agent against Babylon and to be the one who let God's people return from Babylon to the Promised Land (2 Chron. 36:14–23).

The problem of evil in the world lies not with a God in whom "mercy and truth have met together; righteousness and peace have kissed" (Ps. 85:10) but with a humanity that is sinful from its mother's womb (Ps. 51:5), even from Eve and Adam. The solution is not in redefining God but in receiving the salvation He provides through His Son, our Savior.

The Times of the Book of Joshua

The book of Joshua is not an idealized reconstruction of the past. It includes the miraculous, but it also lays bare the failures of individuals, of tribes, and of Israel as a whole. At the same time, many facts about Canaanite history are left unmentioned, facts available only through archaeology and the ancient records found there and in the surrounding areas.

It is crucial to remember that the Old Testament does not purport to be world history, not even the history of Israel in the strict sense of the word, but *covenant history.* It is therefore highly selective in its choice of the material used to tell how salvation came to earth. Gauged by this standard, a conquering campaign by a world empire may be a mere trifle in comparison with the piling up of a few stones to form an altar at Shechem. Therefore, scholars cannot always fit this covenant history into the framework of concomitant circumstances in secular history. Some questions must remain unanswered.

The silence regarding Egypt poses one such problem. Joshua makes not one mention of Pharaoh and his men in spite of Egypt's earlier subjugation of Canaan, the incorporation of Canaan into the empire, and the repeated forays by Egypt into Canaan, even after Egypt had lost the earlier and more effective control of this territory. In fact, Egypt isn't mentioned in the Scriptures at all between the Exodus and the time of Solomon.[7]

One possible solution: Campaigns by Egypt at this time followed the highway up the coastal and through the inland plains, whereas Israel's initial foothold remained restricted to the high-

---

[7]Some scholars have seen at least a veiled reference to the Egyptians in Joshua 24:12: "I sent the hornet before you which drove them out from before you." The word translated "hornet" occurs elsewhere only in Ex. 23:28 and Deut. 7:20. In all three instances, the same thought is expressed, and the definite article is used with the singular noun. In this view, the Egyptian conquest of Canaan prior to Joshua's time would have softened up the land before Israel's entry.

Very likely, the word means "discouragement" or "panic" and is parallel to the fear or terror of God mentioned as a parallel thought in the verse preceding the Exodus passage: "I will send My fear before you, I will cause confusion among all the people to whom you come" (Ex. 23:27).

land ridge. Therefore, the Egyptians also may have been one of the reasons the tribes did not dispossess the cities in the plains. God, of course, could have destroyed them during Joshua's time just as He had at Moses' time if Israel had trusted Him to do so. "One man of you shall chase a thousand, for the LORD your God is He who fights for you, as He promised you" (Joshua 23:10). Fact plus faith makes history stranger than fiction.

The apparently premature reference to the Philistines also presents a problem. Extra-Biblical sources state that the main body of these sea peoples settled on the southern coast of Canaan after 1200 B.C. (cf. "Philistines," chapter 2). Although the book of Joshua mentions no clash with these newcomers, it does refer to "the territory of the Philistines" as one of several areas that remain to be possessed after Joshua's death (13:1–2). But it was more than a century after Joshua's death before the Philistines were in a position to defend their regions against Israel's attempt to dispossess them. For similar proleptic references to the Philistines, see Ex. 13:17 and 23:31.

• • • • •

What Joshua, son of Nun, achieved has meaning only as a preparation for and a promise of Jesus[8], son of Mary and Son of God. The land conquered by Joshua was a perishable inheritance, but Jesus, the mediator of the new covenant, provided "an inheritance incorruptible and undefiled and that does not fade away, reserved in heaven for you" (1 Peter 1:4). "The gospel . . . is the guarantee of our inheritance until the redemption of the purchased possession" (Eph. 1:13–14). But as in Israel's day, "[no] unclean person . . . has any inheritance in the kingdom of Christ and God" (Eph. 5:5).

Therefore, together with Joshua, God's people of every age must and can renew their covenant with God, saying, "As for me and my house, we will serve the LORD" (Joshua 24:15).

---

[8]The names Joshua and Jesus are the same—the former in Hebrew, the latter in Greek.

9. Judges

THE DARK AGES OF ISRAEL

Under Joshua's leadership, the future had looked bright and optimistic. Israel was well on the way to claiming possession of its inheritance. Faithful to God and obedient to Joshua, His covenant representative, the unified tribes had broken the power of vastly superior forces in Canaan. What had been begun (and achieved) by united action and the power of a common faith could be expected to be completed when each tribe, in the same faith and obedience to the covenant, made its way into its allotted territory.

The obstacles facing each tribe were as formidable and insurmountable as the opposition in the days of Joshua. Yet walls as high as those of Jericho would give way, and chariots of iron like those of Jabin (Joshua 11:1–9) would be destroyed by an army lacking even shield or spear (Judg. 5:8). Encouraged and fortified by the miracles of faith in the past, Israel could expect to march on to complete victory.

But those bright prospects vanish, and dark disappointment settles over Israel in the book of Judges. No tribe succeeded in driving out the inhabitants and fully occupying its assigned land. Instead, territory was lost. One tribe (Dan) was entirely dispossessed (chap. 18) and had to find another area to inhabit. Joshua's last words had warned of this ominous future: "If you forsake the LORD and serve foreign gods, then He will turn and do you harm and consume you, after He has done you good" (Joshua 24:20).

Cause and Effect: Setting the Stage

The opening chapters (1:1–3:6) set the stage for this dismal picture in Israel's history. To connect it with the previous period, the state of affairs at Joshua's death are once more mentioned (2:1–10), and the section elaborates on the covenant cause-and-effect theme of "If I . . . , then you . . . ." God had given success to the first phase of capturing Canaan; now Israel was assigned the task of dispossessing the inhabitants and fully occupying the land.

But the people did not obey the Lord. "They followed other gods; . . . and they provoked the Lord to anger" (Judg. 2:12).

Thus they created for themselves a situation that led to their undoing. "Their gods shall be a snare to you" (v. 3). Israel's lack of faith is the reason that it does not accomplish what God has promised to do for and through the nation.

Such inactivity aroused the displeasure of the Lord (vv. 1–5), and Judges shows to what wickedness this dallying with God's promise led. When Israel does not act aggressively, the sin of omission (due to a lack of faith) leads inevitably to sins of commission, and Israel slides downhill into every vice against God and neighbor, into gross idolatry and wickedness of every kind. "Where there is no revelation [and the Law is ignored], the people cast off restraint" (Prov. 29:18).

So it was that "everyone did what was right in his own eyes" (Judg. 21:25), but what they did was "evil in the sight of the LORD" (2:11). Anarchy prevailed. Religious, social, political, and moral principles disappeared. Civil war broke out (chap. 20). These were dark ages indeed for Israel.

The Period of the Judges

These evil days came on Israel soon after Joshua's death when the people had no appointed national leader who could focus their unity. The cohesion of the tribes consisted in their spiritual allegiance to the Lord, the one God. Families made up clans; clans made up tribes; tribes made up a united congregation of worshipers.

By this chain of command from family heads up to tribal leaders, the Mosaic provisions for national life were to be implemented. The covenant alone, its constitution, unified Israel's religious and national life. So long as there was faith in God, the governmental functions would be executed.

SERVING FOREIGN GODS

By breaking the seemingly innocuous command to "make no covenant with the inhabitants of this land" (2:2; cf. Ex. 23:32), Israel began its downfall. God's stipulation was not capricious, nor was it based on narrow-minded racism. Israel was to be His arm of justice against peoples whose measure of wickedness was full and overflowing.

Fraternization and intermarriage with idolaters led to idolatry. The chain reaction of unbelief continued as Israel "forsook the LORD God of their fathers . . . [and] followed other gods from among the gods of the people who were all around them . . . and served Baal and the Ashtoreths" (2:12–13) and "the gods of Syria, the gods of Sidon, the gods of Moab, the gods of the people of Ammon, and the gods of the Philistines" (10:6).

Baalism proved attractive to Israel particularly at this point in its history. When Israel's nomadic way of life gave way to a sedentary agricultural economy, the fertility worship of Baal seemed to offer an abundance of crops, increase in flocks, and the birth of the next generation. Some Israelites even doubted whether the Deliverer from Egypt had divine jurisdiction in Canaan, or whether the land belonged to the local Baal, whose prerogative it was (as the Canaanites assured the Israelite newcomers) to grant the necessary grain and cattle.

Indications are that Israel first rationalized a "small" accommodation to the first commandment: they would continue to worship Yahweh but would do so through the forms of Baalism. But such syncretism denies in theory and practice the one and only God, who had already prescribed the forms of worship and who had already limited worship of Him to the place(s) He would designate. Accommodation to Baalism, a "peaceful coexistence" with it, seemed to grassroots Israel a practical way to assure a livelihood.

In addition, the sensual and sensuous ingredients of Baal worship were seductive and enticing compared to the austere and imageless rites required for Yahweh.

What began as a small accommodation ran amok. When the people rejected God, they also rejected loving their neighbors—and ultimately abused them. That progression may seem a long way down, but Judges teaches that it can be a tiny step. (Cf. the men of the city of Ophrah who were willing to kill Gideon because he had destroyed his father's altar to Baal; 6:25–30.)

Once Baalism had taken root, it was difficult to eradicate. Centuries later, the prophets still were condemning Israel for this idolatry (e.g., 1 Kings 16:31; Jer. 2:8).

If only Israel had remembered the words of Moses: "Hear, O Israel: The LORD our God, the LORD is one!" (Deut. 6:4)

GOD'S PATIENCE

God gave Israel a long time (about 350 years, the period of the judges) to live as a covenant nation without a national representative to preserve its unity.

But lack of faith repeatedly dissolved the nation's bond and resulted in confusion and defeat. Each time that happened, God called Israel back to orderly covenant living. He chose men from various tribes to correct the disorders that had arisen and to give the tribes an opportunity to make a fresh start. But neither severity nor kindness on the part of God succeeded. After such attempts, "the children of Israel [again] did evil in the sight of the

Lord" (Judg. 2:11 et al.). Sadly, Judges is the episodic recital of Israel's failures to live as a theocracy.

We marvel at God's patience. We tire of reading the recurring pattern of (1) gross infidelity, (2) repentance under chastisement, (3) relief from disaster under a deliverer (a "judge"), and (4) the inevitable relapse into the same evil. But every true formula and recapitulation of history must contain the monotonous, unimaginative, and unvarying perversity of the human heart—*and the unending justice and mercy of God.*

The Judges and God, the Judge

Before looking at the individual judges, the reader needs to keep in mind that the Lord Himself is the true Judge of Israel and of all the nations. Therefore, when Israel ran after other gods, He judged them as guilty of breaking the covenant. Yet because of His promise to Israel never to "break My covenant with you" (v. 1), He chastised His people in an attempt to reestablish covenant relations with them. When Israel was brought to its senses by these afflictions, "the LORD raised up judges who delivered them out of the hand of those who plundered them" (v. 16).

To call these deliverers "judges" may seem strange. But as the judge Jephthah pointed out, he was merely the instrument of God's decision to redress the grievance of Israel: "May the LORD, the Judge, render judgment this day between the children of Israel and the people of Ammon" (11:27). Thus by their military campaigns, the judges of Israel put into effect what the supreme Judge had established: the rightful prerogative of Israel to live as His covenant people among the nations.

The covenant also granted each Israelite rights as an individual. So in some instances the task of the judges is specifically mentioned as including the application of God's justice within the nation. Deborah, for example, "would sit under the palm tree of Deborah. . . . And the children of Israel came up to her for judgment" (4:5).

God reserved for Himself the selection and calling of the judges, and the book expressly mentions that they arose at the prompting of the Spirit of God (cf. e.g., 3:9–10). But some, eyeing the national leadership of the peoples surrounding Israel, wanted to make the office of judge hereditary. One judge's son agreed (Gideon's son, Abimelech; 9:1–6), but he ruled only a short time. Normally after God ended the work of the judge, the administration of God's justice again reverted to the regular application of covenant procedures.

THE INDIVIDUAL JUDGES

The space devoted to the various judges (from a sentence or two to multiple chapters) in no way denotes their relative importance. As in earlier history, God has chosen to have certain events recorded as instruction for the faithful and has chosen to omit others. Bible scholars, for their own convenience, have classified the judges as "major" and "minor" according to the amount of space devoted to each. The twelve judges[1] are:

Major Judges	Minor Judges
1. Othniel (3:6–11)—against Mesopotamia	
2. Ehud (3:12–30)—against Moab	
	1. Shamgar (3:31)
3. Barak/Deborah (chaps. 4–5)—against Canaanites under Jabin of Hazor	
4. Gideon (chaps. 6–8)—against Midianites, Amalekites, and people of the east	
	2. Tola (10:1–2)
	3. Jair (10:3–5)
5. Jephthah (10:6–12:7)—against Ammonites	
	4. Ibzan (12:8–10)
	5. Elon (12:11–12)
	6. Abdon (12:13–15)
6. Samson (chaps. 13–16)—against Philistines	
(7. Eli [cf. 1 Sam. 4:18])	
(8. Samuel [cf. 1 Sam. 7:15])	

JUDGING THE JUDGES

As in the case of other Old Testament heroes, the account of these saviors of Israel does not hesitate to expose their clay feet. Some of them are reported to have lapsed into moral and religious aberrations as reprehensible as those they were to correct. Sam-

---

[1]The number of judges is debatable. For example, Shamgar is not explicitly referred to as a judge. Some scholars include Abimelech, Gideon's son, as a judge, though he was chosen by the Israelites as king without divine sanction. Others give the title "judge" to both Barak and Deborah, who worked in concert. And finally, although Samuel is designated as a judge in 1 Sam. 7:6, one may question listing him along with those in the book of Judges.

son inflicted losses on the Philistines, but he fell victim to his own passions (chaps. 13—16). Gideon pulled down the altar of Baal in his father's house and cut down the wooden image beside it (6:25–27) but later perverted the worship of the Lord. Gideon also used booty taken from the enemy to make into an ephod[2], "and all Israel played the harlot with it there. It became a snare to Gideon" (8:23–27; cf. 17:5; 18:14–20).

Jephthah vowed to offer up as a burnt offering whatever came out of the doors of his house to meet him on his victorious return from battle with the Ammonites. When his own daughter met him, Jephthah "carried out his vow with her" (11:29–40). Because of the reference to bewailing her virginity (vv. 37–40), some interpreters believe that Jephthah commuted the death sentence to life-long celibacy.[3]

The Book of Judges

GOD'S PURPOSE FOR ISRAEL

God had one purpose in creating Israel and giving Canaan as an inheritance. In His covenant with the patriarchs and with Israel at Mount Sinai, He had made it clear that Israel was to be a means to an end: to bring the blessings of salvation to all nations.

God had His own inscrutable reason for electing Israel as the chosen nation, but He reveals some of the reasons why He directed the course of Israel's history at the time of the conquest as He did.

He would, first of all, give Israel physical possession of the land in a way most advantageous to the conquerors: "The LORD your God will drive out those nations . . . little by little, . . . lest the beasts of the field become too numerous" (Deut. 7:22; cf. Ex. 23:29–30).

This pattern of gradual conquest also committed Israel to learn to be true spiritual heirs of the land. During such a pro-

---

[2]"Ephod," a transliteration from the Hebrew, seems to be applied to various objects in the Old Testament. In Ex. 28:6–14 and 39:2–7, it designates an upper garment of the high priest. A linen ephod is also worn by the general priests (cf. 1 Sam. 2:18; 2 Sam. 6:14; et al.). Gideon's and Micah's ephods (Judg. 8:23–27; 17:5) appear to be metal images. (In Hebrew, the words for "ephod" and "ark" are similar, and scribes may have confused them in copying the texts.) Thus Gideon may have made his own ark to be worshiped.

Whatever Gideon made, his action at best worshiped Yahweh by means of an idolatrous rite.

[3]In view of Jephthah's ungodly action, it cannot be ruled out a priori that he may have lapsed into the Canaanite/Moabite practice of child sacrifice. Cf. Walter R. Roehrs and Martin H. Franzmann, *Concordia Self-Study Commentary* (St. Louis: Concordia Publishing House, 1973), p. 171.

tracted period, they could conquer only by faith and in obedience to the covenant. Only as "a kingdom of priests" (Ex. 19:6) were they to displace the kings of Canaan.

The people had ample opportunity to learn this lesson. But after Joshua's death Israel lacked the faith to be God's covenant nation and thus did not dispossess the Canaanites.[4]

God did not deviate from His announced program for Israel. As long as the Canaanites remained, they served to "test Israel by them, to know whether [Israel] would obey the commandments of the LORD, which He had commanded their fathers by the hand of Moses" (Judg. 3:4). This situation remained for a long time, as can be seen from the book of Judges. Even a new generation, which "had not known any of the wars in Canaan" (v. 1), was not permitted to possess the land without learning to wage war as God's people (i.e., to conquer by faith in Him and for His ends).

OUTLINE

The arrangement of the material in this book apparently follows a progression. The movement begins with the setting of the sun of faith and ends in the midnight of moral and religious chaos.

Chapters 1:1–3:6

This introduction leads the reader to expect an unpleasant chapter in the history of the covenant nation. Evil days are to follow Joshua's death for two reasons.
1. The tribes of Israel lacked the faith to complete the conquest of Canaan (1:1–2:5). But without the faith of a covenant nation, Israel has no claim to the land. Nor will God "drive them out before you; but they shall be thorns in your side, and their gods shall be a snare to you" (2:3). Israel wept at the prospect but did not stir itself to resolute acts of faith.
2. Israel's default of faith made it a victim of the circumstances it had created (2:6–3:6). The remaining Canaanites tempted Israel into overt acts of disobedience against God. Because "they forsook the LORD and served Baal and the Ashtoreths, . . . He delivered them into the hands of plunderers who despoiled them. . . . [Thus] wherever they went out, the hand of the LORD was against them for calamity" (2:13–15). A preview is then given of the period to

---

[4]Two of the few successful tribal leaders were Caleb, Joshua's fellow spy into Canaan under Moses, and Othniel, Caleb's younger brother (1:11–20).

follow. Periodic deliverance from these oppressions did not rouse Israel to a heroism of faith but resulted only in relapses into the same unholy living.

Chapters 3:7–16:31

In this main body of the book, specific examples document the thematic introduction and characterization of this period. Light and shadow alternate almost as regularly as day and night. Sin and its depressing consequences are repeatedly listed as necessitating the judges for deliverance—but sin always returns.

The following description of the events involving the first judge, Othniel (3:7–11), serves to summarize the recurring story:

> So Israel did evil in the sight of the LORD. Therefore the anger of the LORD was hot against Israel, and He sold them into the hand [of an enemy]. When Israel cried out to the LORD, the LORD raised up a deliverer for Israel, who delivered them. The Spirit of the Lord came upon him, and he judged Israel. He went out to war, and the Lord delivered [the enemy] into his hand. So the land had rest. Then [the deliverer] died. And Israel again did evil in the sight of the Lord.

Chapters 17–21

In painting this era as Israel's dark ages, the artist has reserved his darkest hues for the last chapters. The two episodes recorded here could have happened at any time during the period. But by placing them at the end of the book, the author creates a climactic effect and records how far Israel went into the night of sin. At the same time, this arrangement lets trust in God's mercy mount in direct proportion to the evil. To penitent Israel God's promise remained: "I will never break My covenant with you" (2:1)

1. The first vignette (chaps. 17–18) portrays particularly how far Israel went in perverting the true worship of God. Even a Levite, possibly a priest, prostitutes his office to erect idolatrous images. Love of money and ease had stifled his love for God.

2. The second picture (chaps. 19–21) appears even more revolting. A Levite and his concubine/wife, traveling home through the territory of Benjamin, stopped in Gibeah for the night. There the men of the city wanted the traveler for homosexual purposes. The Levite and his host gave the girl to the men of the city for their pleasure. They raped her throughout the night, and in the morning she was found dead outside the door. The days of Sodom and Gomorrah had returned. The only ray of light in this Stygian darkness is that Israel as a whole had enough sense of

right and wrong to be called into a concerted action to punish the offenders.

THE TRIBAL ATTEMPTS EVALUATED

Six tribes receive completely negative reports: Zebulon, Asher, Naphtali, Manasseh, Ephraim, and Dan (1:27–34).

In an unusual reference to the House of Joseph (Manasseh and Ephraim), the city of Bethel is captured (vv. 22–26), but nothing is said of permanent possession of either the city or its territory.

The tribe of Judah receives a fuller account in Judges (as it did in Joshua), though it is still sketchy. This tribe fared better than the others in taking possession. As a contributing factor, the tribe of Simeon cooperated in victory at Bezek (vv. 1–7) and Zephath (v. 17). Two Judaites who feared the Lord, Caleb and his younger brother Othniel, also successfully took the cities of Debir (vv. 11–15) and Hebron (v. 20), although credit for the latter is given in verse 10 to the whole tribe of Judah. In spite of these victories, Judah "took possession [only] of the hill country, but he could not drive out the inhabitants of the plain, because they had chariots of iron" (v. 19 RSV).

The tribe of Benjamin is mentioned in immediate connection with Judah (v. 21). Although this reference mentions that "the children of Benjamin did not drive out the Jebusites who inhabited Jerusalem," Joshua 15:63 attributes the failure to Judah. Since Benjamin and Judah had contiguous borders, both tribes evidently tried to take possession of this important city. Nothing in Joshua or Judges precludes united onslaughts against Jerusalem[5] sometimes led by Benjamin and sometimes by Judah.

Having told in chapter 1 how it came about that Israel's conquest was incomplete, the writer proceeds in chapter 2 to describe the consequences: Israel by its own lack of faith was about to be "Canaanized" and lose its mission as God's instrument of salvation to the nations. Therefore, since their occupation of Canaan would no longer serve His purposes, "[God] will no longer drive out before them any of the nations which Joshua left when he died" (2:21). But He did not abandon His people forever. God let their enemies afflict them, and when Israel repented, He would send a deliverer, a judge (2:11–19).

---

[5]Although 1:8 reports that Judah took Jerusalem, the people evidently were not dispossessed from it, for the city was not conquered permanently until David (2 Sam. 5:6–9).

THE TIME SPAN OF JUDGES

Because the book is episodic, it is hard to reckon the actual lapse of time. The book does list the time of persecution preceding the six major judges as well as the time of rest after their deliverance. But with the exception of Shamgar, it lists only the duration of the judgeship of each minor judge.

Although the years given in the book total only 410 years[6], 1 Kings 6:1 gives a total of 480 years[7] from "after the children of Israel had come out of the land of Egypt" (about 1440 B.C.) and the fourth year of Solomon (968 B.C.). After subtracting time for Eli, Samuel, Saul, and David, only about 300 years remain for the judges. A number of factors allow for this reduction.

One need not assume from Scripture that the events of Judges took place consecutively rather than simultaneously. For example, the phrase "The Lord . . . sold them into the hands of the Philistines and into the hands of the people of Ammon" (Judg. 10:7) may introduce both Jephthah's deliverance from the Ammonites (10:6–12:7) and Samson's forays against the Philistines (chaps. 13–16).

With one exception, all the periods of rest and one of oppression are reckoned in terms of 40 years (i.e., a generation) or a multiple of it. No doubt some of these are round figures denoting a generation.

Jephthah, the second-last judge, reminds the Ammonites (in 11:26) that some 300 years had passed since they suffered defeat under Moses.

· · · · ·

Joshua—Judges—Jesus

Although Joshua is not specifically called a judge, the judges are called "joshuas" (i.e., saviors). They did their part to keep open the channels of the covenant "that we should be saved from our enemies and from the hand of all who hate us" (Luke 1:71). But they merely paved the way for the coming of *the* Joshua, the Savior, Joshua/Jesus of Nazareth.

More wonderful in birth than Samson, perfect in obedience beyond all these saviors of Israel, Jesus did more than lead the fray against the enemies of humanity; He directed the full brunt

---

[6]The total includes 111 years of oppression and the major judges, 70 years of the minor judges, 226 years of rest, and 3 years of Abimelech.

[7]Paul mentions in round figures that God "gave them judges for about four hundred and fifty years" (Acts 13:20). No doubt he is referring to the years of the judges in their totality.

of their attack on Himself to His own death. It was no futile act of desperation like that of Samson; the Lord rose from the grave in triumph over the vanquished foe.

The result: Not rest merely for a generation or two, but endless rest.

10. Ruth

The book of Ruth supplements Judges in several ways. It records a bit of delightful covenant history of that period and supplies further evidence of the faithfulness of God to His promises.

The scope of the story is not national or tribal as is Judges. It is limited to individuals, and the plot is laid within the confines of family life. What happens to this little covenant family in its domestic struggles concerns God as much as the big issues of national survival.

When the heroine of the story "happened to come" to a certain field (2:3), God was giving her a chance to reap the reward of faith and faithfulness. She had not in vain taken refuge under the wings of Israel's God (v. 12). At the right juncture of small circumstances, God prepared a man to spread his wing of protection over her (3:9). [1]

The story of Ruth also portrays the exception to the general picture of anarchy and lawlessness during the time of the judges. Then as always, a faithful remnant lived in Israel—wholesome, decent, magnanimous people. Home ties were close; marriage was sacred; purity and restraint of passions had not vanished. If family life was sound, albeit by exception, Israel could hope for national healing and health.

The book of Ruth, which could be called "A Rose Growing Out of the Muck of Iniquity," thus provides dramatic relief from the strain of general horror and savagery of the period of the judges.

The Account of Ruth

Commentators vie with one another in praising form and content of this masterful short story, known by the heroine's name, Ruth. In reality, her mother-in-law, Naomi, plays the most significant role of the drama.

Because of a famine, Naomi's husband had taken her and their two sons from Bethlehem to "sojourn in the country of Moab" (1:1). After the death of her husband and two sons, Naomi planned to return to Judah, for the famine was now over (v. 6). Ruth, the Moabite widow of one of Naomi's sons, insisted on casting her lot with Naomi and Naomi's God. So the stage was set for the main plot of the story, leading to a happy ending: the marriage of Ruth

---

[1]The Hebrew word for "wing" (2:12) and "garment" (3:9) is the same.

to Boaz. "Wise as serpents and harmless as doves" (Matt. 10:16), Naomi directed Ruth's "chance" acquaintance with prosperous Boaz. In guileless simplicity, Ruth followed Naomi's instructions, and Naomi's trust in Boaz's integrity, kindness, and sense of duty to the extended family was not misplaced.

The book of Ruth is not merely or primarily a love story but covenant history, albeit on a small scale. Naomi, Ruth, and Boaz knew and responded in faith to the promises and provisions of Israel's God. The son born to Boaz and Ruth, Obed, became the heir of her previous husband and his clan. To indicate Ruth's and Boaz's compliance with this stipulation, the child was given to Naomi and reckoned as her son (Ruth 4:13–17).

At the same time, this family anecdote flows like a small rivulet into the main stream of larger covenant history. Ruth became the great-grandmother of David, from whom issued great David's greater Son, born at Bethlehem to fulfill all covenant promises (4:21–22; cf. 1 Chron. 2:12–15; Matt. 1:5–6).

ANCIENT PRACTICES

Although the story is simple, the modern reader needs an acquaintance with four laws and customs of that day in order to understand the development of the plot.

1. Naomi and Ruth use their covenant right of the poor to glean in someone else's field at harvesttime (cf. Lev. 19:9; 23:22; Deut. 24:19). This was necessary after they returned from Moab either because the ancestral field had not been sown or because its crop belonged to someone else. Note the words of Boaz (Ruth 4:3), "Naomi . . . sold the piece of land which belonged to our brother Elimelech."

2. The main action of the book hinges on the duties of the kinsman. Covenant legislation provided for "redemption" of land sold by an impoverished relative (Lev. 25:23–28). "Anyone who is near of kin[2] to him" (Lev. 25:49) had this obligation.

3. Mosaic law also decreed the so-called levirate marriage (Deut. 25:5–10). The brother-in-law (Latin: *levir*) was required to marry the widow of a childless marriage. Custom seems to have extended this statute to apply to more distant relatives as well. Neither Boaz nor the relative closer than he (Ruth 3:12) was the brother-in-law of Ruth, yet

---

[2]The frequent Hebrew word in Ruth translated "relative" is related to the verb "to redeem" and the noun "redemption." A "redeeming relative" fulfilled his duty as a relative by delivering or saving the needy one from his or her predicament.

the latter agreed to act as the "deliverer" of the property. But when Boaz informed the other relative of the duty also to play the part of a *levir*, he backed off, leaving Boaz free to buy "all that was Elimelech's"—and thereby also to claim the right to marry Ruth (4:9–10).

4. To confirm the release of property rights, the closer kinsman drew off his shoe before witnesses at the gate of the city. This strange custom was based on part of the regulation of Deut. 25:8–10 concerning the public repudiation of one who refused to perform the duty of the *levir*. In that case, the widow drew off the relative's shoe and spat in his face, perhaps to shame him (or another relative) into compliance.

THE TIME OF THE STORY

According to Ruth 1:1, these things happened "in the days when the judges ruled," but only two generations before the time of David; for Obed (Ruth's son) was "the father of Jesse, the father of David" (4:17). Very likely, this family story took place during the time of Eli, with which the books of Samuel open.

The genealogy from Perez to David (vv. 18–22) no doubt is only partial. Salmon, the sixth link, who married Rahab after the fall of Jericho (cf. Matt. 1:5) perhaps some 250–300 years earlier, was probably a genealogical "father" of Boaz.

THE POINT OF THE STORY

This lovely idyll portrays the blessings that God in His providence bestows on individuals who live out the covenant, reestablished under Joshua at Shechem, as they promised: "The LORD our God we will serve, and His voice we will obey" (Joshua 24:24).

But one of the main features of the story seems to be in conflict with this conclusion. Boaz's marriage to a Moabite woman seems not to conform to the covenant specification in Deut. 7:3, which prohibited marriage with non-Israelite women. On the other hand, intermarriage with Moabites was not expressly forbidden in this passage. Although Deut. 23:3 states that "an Ammonite or a Moabite shall not enter the congregation of the LORD, even to the tenth generation," this prohibition may not refer to intermarriage but to the exclusion of male Moabites from worship rites.

In any event, God's laws were designed to keep Israel from losing identity as the chosen people of God. There is room in His goodness to acknowledge Ruth's surrender of homeland, nationality, and paganism in her desire to serve the true God of Israel.

Later, after the return of the exiles from Babylonia and at the time of Ezra and Nehemiah, intermarriage of Israelites with "the people of the land" (including Moabites) was a serious problem (Ezra 9:1–4; cf. 10:2–3). Some scholars have concluded that Ruth was written as a historical novel after the return from Babylonia in order to counteract Ezra's prohibitions against mixed marriages. But if the book were a novel, it would have carried no weight at Ezra's time because it improperly attributes "impure blood" to Israel's great King David.

Yet the fact that the story does attribute "impure blood" to Israel's *greatest* king (Matt. 1:5) affirms Jesus as the Savior of all humanity, old covenant and noncovenant people equally.

• • • • •

The book of Ruth, the pericopal reading in the synagogue for the Festival of Weeks (the time of barley harvest), or Pentecost, has its place above all in the New Testament festival of Pentecost. Filled with the Holy Spirit, the apostle Peter proclaimed salvation to Israel and to "all who are afar off, as many as the Lord our God will call" (Acts 2:39). Ruth's good fortune was but a preliminary foreshadowing of that redemption for all.

Boaz redeemed only a parcel of ground, but the "Redeeming Relative" of the fulfillment has restored to humanity an inheritance in heaven by the redemption that He paid with His blood.

11. 1 and 2 Samuel

Covenant History:
"The Sure Mercies of David" (Is. 55:3)

JUDGES PRIOR TO DAVID

The book of Judges documented Israel's repeated failures to function as God's instrument to bring about His covenanted promise of salvation to all people. The bright exception of Ruth only confirmed the general rule of this dark period. And the first part of 1 Samuel seems to be merely another chapter in the record of this dreary state of affairs.

In the opening chapters Israel's dissolution worsened. The Philistines continued as God's scourge on the unfaithful people. Samson's earlier skirmishes had held them in check only temporarily, and after his ignominious death they invaded Israel in force. In fact, Israel's humiliation at their hands reached hitherto unplumbed depths. The Philistines destroyed the center of Israel's worship at Shiloh and bore away as a trophy of war Israel's holiest possession: the Ark of the Covenant (1 Sam. 4:5). The well-ordered and precisely defined worship of the Lord (established at Mount Sinai) could no longer be maintained.[1]

God's extreme punitive measure was provoked by a progressive breakdown of religious and moral rectitude that reached even into the highest places: the family of the high priest, Eli. His sons, one of whom was destined to hold this most sacred position, "had no regard for the LORD, . . . treated the offering of the LORD with contempt, . . . [and] lay with the women who served at the entrance to the tent of meeting" (2:12–22 RSV).

As before, God raised up a judge to deliver Israel from the Philistines. So important was his activity that the records of this and the succeeding periods are identified by his name: Samuel. He "judged Israel all the days of his life" (7:15).

But these dreary opening chapters also betoken a better day. Samuel's weapon of deliverance was not strength of arms but the power of prayer; he "cried out to the LORD for Israel, and the LORD answered him" (7:9).

Like Moses and like the prophets who would arise later, Sam-

---

[1]In this emergency, as at other times during the judges, altars were erected at various places where the Lord caused His name to dwell (Ex. 20:24).

117

uel was an intercessor (cf. Jer. 15:1). As a mediator of the word of the Lord, he called Israel back to covenant faithfulness. At his urging, "the children of Israel put away the Baals and the Ashtoreths, and served the LORD only" (1 Sam. 7:4).

But the change was not complete; so Samuel tried by an unprecedented move to continue it until it became permanent. When he "was old . . . he made his sons judges over Israel. . . . But his sons did not walk in his ways; they turned aside after dishonest gain, took bribes, and perverted justice" (8:1–3).

Nevertheless, this judge and prophet helped restore Israel in its role as God's chosen people. At God's behest he supplied Israel with permanent leadership in the person of a king, first Saul and then David. Under the former, order was restored only partially and temporarily. At his death the Philistines controlled more Israelite territory than before and seemed to have all the Promised Land in their grip.

But Samuel also had anointed David to be the next king in Israel. This "man after His [God's] own heart" (13:14) again made Israel the instrument of God's holy purposes. The reversal of conditions during David's reign was nothing short of miraculous. Chaos gave way to order, disintegration and dissolution to stability, degradation and disgrace to Israel's golden age of glory. This physical and spiritual reestablishment of the covenant people is the story of the two books of Samuel.

THE MONARCHY IN ISRAEL

God had chosen Israel "to be a people for Himself, a special treasure [KJV: "a peculiar people"] above all the peoples who are on the face of the earth," to be "a holy people to the LORD your God" and "a kingdom of priests" (Deut. 14:2; 26:19; Ex. 19:6). Its holiness, which made it different from the other nations, was to be above all its *spiritual* relationship with God through faith.

But also its political administration was to be different. All the nations around Israel were governed by kings; Israel alone had been the exception. In Egypt and in the Tigris and Euphrates Valley absolute monarchies held sway, some as incarnate sons of the gods. Even the small city-states in Canaan were headed by autocratic kings. Significantly, it was not so in Israel. Their king was "the LORD of hosts."[2]

Israel's form of government is called a *theocracy.* In the cov-

---

[2]The expression "the LORD *zebaoth,*" ("LORD of hosts" or "armies") occurs for the first time in Scripture on the lips of Samuel's mother, Hannah (1 Sam. 1:11).

enant, *God* had provided for Israel's government. *His* statutes were to promote and establish internal order. *The Lord of hosts* would direct the people in battle through leaders especially appointed for the exigencies of the moment. And *God* had commissioned Israel as a tribal confederacy to complete the conquest of Canaan after the death of Joshua.

Yet Israel became a monarchy after centuries of existence without a king because of its lack of faith in its true King, the Lord of hosts. After Joshua, the individual tribes failed to take God at His word; they did not trust His promise of help in taking full possession of the land. God tried for a long time—the whole period of the judges—to call Israel back to live by faith in His promises. Instead, Israel repeatedly sank close to being just another secular people like those around them. Israel sold its birthright for the pottage of Canaan's materialism and sensual worship. In spite of the judges' frequent deliverance of Israel from punishment at the hands of its enemies, a thorough change of heart did not result. Israel always reverted to its common pattern, and always the Lord "delivered them into the hands of plunderers" (Judg. 2:14). Chaos would reign again, and the Philistines threatened to engulf the nation.

Israel tried to escape this situation of its own making not by the repentance and faith of a people of God but by being still more like the Canaanites: "Make for us a king to judge us *like all the nations*" (1 Sam. 8:5, emphasis added). "The thing displeased Samuel" (v. 6). He recognized their request for what it was: a rejection of God's help in favor of human security, the desire to live by sight rather than by faith.

God answered their request with an emphatic no. God would not let His people become "Canaanized" and secularized. He would not give them a king as a substitute for Himself and so let them reject Him. At the same time He instructed Samuel "to heed their voice" (v. 9).[3] Long-suffering in the face of Israel's unwillingness to rise to the challenge of its destiny, He would come to the aid of its weak faith by giving it a visible and tangible representative of His rule, of *His* kingship, in the person of a human king.

Scripture gives abundant evidence that God did not relinquish His rule to an earthly king and let Israel be "like all the nations." First, Israel would not crown men on the basis of their proven abilities. God Himself chose Saul and David, obscure and

---

[3]God's view of Israel's request had not changed. When Israel gathered at Mizpah to select the first king, Samuel reminded the people once more that in their desire for a king (motivated as it was) they in fact had rejected God (1 Sam. 10:17–19).

untried men, and directed Samuel to find them and to anoint them for office. Second, God would permit no glorification or cult of the king. The king's person had no status except as the mediating executive of the covenant. He would rule in God's name, by God's Spirit, and for God's purposes. Third, one law applied to both king and subjects: covenant fidelity. In battle, for example, "the LORD does not save with sword and spear" (17:47), and neither would the king. Victory would be assured only "if both you [the people] and the king . . . will follow the LORD your God; . . . but if you will not hearken to the voice of the LORD, but rebel against the commandment of the LORD, then the hand of the LORD will be against you and your king" (12:14–15 RSV).

The monarchy, different from a tribal confederacy of course, would result in outward changes of administration. Samuel called attention to these (8:10–18): concentration of power in the hands of a king, conscription of armed forces from all the tribes, requisition of national resources, and taxation for the support of the court and its administrative offices. And there was no guarantee that succeeding kings would not abuse their power and make oppressive and arbitrary demands on their subjects (as later history proved they did).

Samuel tried to forestall such autocratic evils. Because the king was bound to rule within the framework of the established covenant, Samuel specified "the rights and duties of the kingship; and he wrote them in a book[4] and laid it up before the LORD" (10:25 RSV).

Such was the monarchy that God permitted Israel to have. But even this concession to Israel's weak faith did not bring about a greater loyalty and faithfulness to God in its covenant relationship. The next historical books of the Old Testament, the books of the kings, bring the sad news of Israel's persistent disobedience under the monarchy, the collapse of the royal house, and the complete loss of the Promised Land.

Covenant Blessings Under the Monarchy

Nevertheless, God used the monarchy (particularly the reign of David) to reestablish Israel as His covenant nation in order to carry forward His ultimate purpose: to bring His mercy to all nations. This rehabilitation was effected in all areas of Israel's life.

Full possession of the land would be theirs as God carried out His promise. What Joshua had not completed and what the

---

[4]This document no doubt incorporated and elaborated the terms set down in Deut. 17:14–20.

individual tribes lacked the faith to do was achieved under David. All opposition of the Canaanites was overcome, and the land "from the river of Egypt to the great river, the River Euphrates" (Gen. 15:18) finally became Israel's possession. David's kingdom extended even beyond the borders of Canaan proper and took on the proportions of an empire.

Moral order was restored. No longer could anyone do "what was right in his own eyes" (Judg. 21:25) as in the days of the judges. Covenant ethics were again enforced. Justice prevailed, for the king himself supervised and supplemented the judicial procedures and acted as the court of final appeal. So absolute was the application of justice that not even the king could flout with impunity the rights of his subjects. (E.g., David's murder and adultery did not go uncondemned and unpunished.)

Under such conditions, **material prosperity** also flourished. The people could sow and harvest in peace. After David's conquests and control of the ancient trade routes, commerce and trade became a new source of wealth. Alongside an agrarian way of life arose an urban and commercial economy.

Also **Israel's worship** eventually was restored to conform more to covenant regulations. During the time of the judges, Israel's disobedience had created conditions that made it impossible to observe the unified and ordered system of worship defined in Mosaic law. In addition, at Samuel's time the Philistines had conquered and destroyed Shiloh (where the sanctuary had been) and had captured the Ark of the Covenant (1 Sam. 4:1–11). During foreign occupation and the absence of the ark, festivals such as the Day of Atonement evidently could not be observed. But God still desired and accepted Israel's worship to the extent that it was sincere and that the people were able to observe Mosaic regulations. Therefore, altars were erected at various places during this confused period, and sacrifices acceptable to God were made (Ex. 20:24).[5]

Under the monarchy conditions gradually returned to the prescribed practice. David brought the ark to Jerusalem and reestablished the priesthood. But he was not destined to build a temple or to reinaugurate the full order of service; God reserved this for David's son Solomon.

Spiritual life was fortified and directed to a greater degree by the prophets. This office was not new to Israel; both Moses and

---

[5]No arbitrary disregard was permissible, however. Saul's assumption of priestly functions was severely punished (1 Sam. 13:11–14), as was the profaning of the ark (6:19). Cf. 15:22: "Behold, to obey is better than sacrifice, and to heed than the fat of rams."

Joshua had been spokesmen of God to Israel (although the latter is not expressly called a prophet). During the time of the judges "the LORD sent a prophet [unnamed] to the children of Israel" (Judg. 6:8). Furthermore, a human mediator likely is meant in Judg. 10:11: "The LORD said to the children of Israel. . . ." Samuel was also "established as a prophet of the LORD" (e.g., 1 Sam. 3:20; 15:10).

In addition, Scripture tells of "companies" or "bands of prophets" and "sons of prophets" (cf. 1 Kings 20:35; 2 Kings 2:3; for Samuel's involvement, see also 1 Sam. 10:11; 19:20). Apparently living a communal life, these sons (pupils) were under the tutelage of a "father," a supervisor, for their instruction in the word of the Lord (cf. 2 Kings 2:12). When the Spirit of God came on them, they were seized by an ecstatic frenzy and "prophesied" in utterances perhaps similar to the phenomenon known in the New Testament as speaking in tongues. Even an outsider to the group, Saul, was twice overcome by the same manifestation of the Spirit when he ventured into their company "and he prophesied" (1 Sam. 10:6–13; 19:23–24; cf. Num. 11:24–29).[6]

We are not told of these groups' other activities. No doubt they studied the Word of the Lord that had come to Israel previously, preserved the words and writings of the prophets, and participated in the services of worship.

David, quoted in the New Testament as a prophet himself (Matt. 27:35), had at his side as counselors the prophets Nathan and Gad.

The prophets played an important part during the entire period of the monarchy—and even after that. Some of them left their messages in the books bearing their names; some did not (cf. Michaiah, 2 Chron. 18:6–27). But all the prophets, differing in temperament and endowments, are cast in the same mold of uncompromising integrity in speaking the oracles of God. Unique in the ancient world, they all insisted that Israel's kings submit to covenant obedience, for God's one standard applied to all people. The doctrines and teachings of the prophets did not vary: "Behold, to obey is better than sacrifice, and to heed than the fat of rams" (1 Sam. 15:22).

The Messianic Kingdom

Because of all these physical and spiritual blessings during Israel's golden age, David's reign became a symbol and prophetic type of the fulfillment of the old covenant in the new: God's prom-

---

[6]For the use of music with prophesy, see 1 Chron. 25:1–8.

ise of a spiritual rule in human hearts. That covenant promise had not changed when the patriarchal system of Abraham changed into a federation of tribes at Sinai, nor did God set a different goal when He permitted the federation to have a monarch to implement the covenant. But now the anointed king (David and his son and offspring) would represent God's rule on earth until from their seed would come the fulfillment of all that they typified so imperfectly: "the Son of God . . . the King of Israel" (John 1:49).

The Hebrew word for "anointed one" is *meshiach*, Messiah (Gk.: *Christos*). The term "messianic prophesy" therefore may be limited to the covenant promises that refer to the Messiah's royalty and His descent from David.[7] But in a wider sense all Old Testament types and promises may be called messianic. Christ established His royal kingdom by absorbing and fulfilling in His person the function of all the Old Testament prototypes of God's rule—the king as well as the prophet, the anointed high priest, the Servant of the Lord, the Son of Man, the Redeemer, and the Man of Sorrows by whose "stripes we are healed" (Is. 53:5).

Because David's kingdom was established within the framework and under the provisions of the covenant, the covenant itself safeguarded the monarchy as a messianic type and did not let it become a rule of "messiahs." Thus Nathan, speaking for the Lord, could say to David, "I will set up your seed after you. . . . I will be his Father, and he shall be My son" (2 Sam. 7:12, 14). Solomon, the messianic type in this passage, was God's son only because the sonship of all Israel was embodied in him (cf. Ex. 4:22–23; Hos. 11:1). But Solomon could not claim to be the incarnation of God (as, for example, the pharaohs did); he was the type pointing to the coming of Him of whom God said, "This is My beloved Son, in whom I am well pleased" (Matt. 3:17 and parallel passages; cf. also Luke 9:35).

Nevertheless, David's kingdom as a messianic type was often misunderstood. Many Israelites expected its fulfillment in an earthly reign in Israel of a still greater man than David. Even the disciples shortly before Christ's ascension asked, "Lord, will You at this time restore the [earthly] kingdom to Israel?" (Acts 1:6) Perhaps to forestall such a misunderstanding, Jesus from the beginning of His ministry called Himself "the Son of Man" rather

---

[7]E.g., Is. 9:6–7; 11:1, 11; Jer. 23:5–6; Ezek. 34:20–24; Amos 9:11–12; Zech. 9:9–10.

than "the Son of David."[8]

Like all prophetic types, David's kingdom was an imperfect vehicle. He stooped to unkingly and unmessianic behavior. His "house," intended to occupy "the throne of his kingdom forever" (2 Sam. 7:13), was swept away by foreign kings. This failure does not impugn God's promise concerning the enduring character of David's dynasty, for the promise was conditioned on the covenant. In spite of Israel's frequent failure to live by the covenant, God kept His promises. "My mercy I will keep for him [David] forever, and My covenant shall stand firm with him" (Ps. 89:28; cf. Is. 55:3; Acts 13:33). And when the time was fulfilled, Mary, the peasant girl of Nazareth, heard the angelic messenger prophesy of her royal son,

> He will be great, and will be called the Son of the Highest; and the Lord God will give Him the throne of His father David. And He will reign over the house of Jacob forever, and of His kingdom there will be no end. (Luke 1:32–33)

The Books of Samuel As Historical Record

The account of the rise of Israel from near extinction to empire glory[9] is unique in ancient national histories. God did not design Scripture to be a national history in the usual sense. The center of interest is not Israel as a state or nation but as God's chosen people and instrument. The sacred record does not report events according to their importance for or glory of the state or king. In fact, decisive battles grudgingly are given a few lines of space while whole pages are devoted to moral and religious issues in the lives of individuals. The selection and elaboration of materials are governed by their value to God's cause-and-effect covenant history. Defeat came to those who frustrated God's purposes, but success crowned the efforts of those who advanced His kingdom. "David became greater and greater, for the LORD, the God of hosts, was with him" (2 Sam. 5:10 RSV).

Because the books of Samuel devote much space to representative individuals under the covenant, the stories throb with human interest and emotion. The loftiest motives of friendship, loyalty, and piety vie against treachery, betrayal, and desecration

---

[8]Jesus did not deny the fulfillment of the Davidic and royal prophecies in Himself when challenged on who He was (Matt. 22:42–45), nor did He repudiate this title when addressed as the Son of David (9:27).

[9]Israel's great change in status from vassalage to empire took place within the span of about a century—Eli: 40 years (1 Sam. 4:18); Samuel: no length of time indicated; Saul: 40 years (Acts 13:21); David: 40 years (2 Sam. 5:4).

of everything sacred. Across this stage of history march villains who are and remain wicked, heroes who fall and cannot rise again, and fallen saints who do repent.

The writer is intent on tracing history and evaluating individuals and events according to their contribution to or hindrance of God's ultimate goal for history. A strict chronological arrangement of events is of only secondary consideration. This disregard of chronology surfaces particularly in the stories of David. His victories over the surrounding nations and those of his administrative personnel, for example, are given brief summaries in 2 Sam. 8. Then one of those victories (over the Ammonites and Syrians, 8:3–12) is given in more detail in chapter 10 and in 12:26–31. The closing chapters (2 Sam. 21–24) also supplement the previous biographical accounts of David. For example, chapter 21 evidently occurred before 2 Sam. 16:8 (in which David is cursed for the action in 21:1–14).

The author, writing as much as a century or more after these events had occurred, no doubt had recourse to various records. In noncovenant nations such annals were written not by free men but by groveling sycophants under the direct control of the king. But Israel's prophets, who by divine authority directed even kings to act in faithful adherence to the covenant, recorded what God did through the nation and through individuals to implement His covenant promises. Thus the author of Samuel likely had before him "the book of Samuel the seer, . . . the book of Nathan the prophet, . . . [and] the book of Gad the seer" (1 Chron. 29:29) and used these sources to achieve his above-stated purpose—a history not of David but of the kingdom of God.

THE BATTLES AND WARS FOR INDEPENDENCE AND POWER

The way to Israel's golden age was a fierce and bloody struggle. Humanly speaking, David's empire could become a reality only because the great powers of the Fertile Crescent were not then (about 1000 B.C.) in a position to extend their domination into Canaan. Egypt had lost control of the area completely; Babylonia's first empire (Hammurabi's) had crumbled; Hittite power had been swept away by peoples from the islands and coasts of the Aegean Sea; Assyria had crushed the Hurrians (founders of the kingdom of Mitanni) but needed a few more centuries to consolidate its gains before becoming the mistress of the ancient world. David, of course, did not create this favorable international situation, but he exploited the providential timing of world events to the full.

As noted, Israel previously had not succeeded in protecting itself against the peoples in and around Canaan. Therefore, pos-

session of its inheritance was an uphill struggle involving disappointments as well as successes. A brief outline of the battles, disastrous and victorious, will help trace the ascent from degradation to glory. (The list is topical, not necessarily chronological).

Campaigns Against the Philistines

A. By Eli:
   Israel defeated twice at Aphek (1 Sam. 4), an unidentified site, perhaps in the Plain of Esdraelon near Jezreel (cf. 1 Sam. 29:1).
B. By Samuel:
   Israel repulsed the Philistines at Mizpah (1 Sam. 7:3–14).
C. By Saul:
   1. Victory with Jonathan's help at Michmash (1 Sam. 13–14).
   2. Pursued the enemy to Gath and Ekron after David slew Goliath at Sochoh (1 Sam. 17:1–52).
   3. Saul's death in the Philistine victory at Mount Gilboa (1 Sam. 28, 31).
D. By David:
   1. Two victories in the valley of Rephaim (south of Jerusalem) and pursuit into enemy territory (2 Sam. 5:17–25).
   2. Victories over individual Philistines by David's men (2 Sam. 21:15–21).
   3. Defeat of the Philistines (2 Sam. 8:1) and capture of Metheg Ammah (perhaps Gath; cf. 1 Chron. 18:1).

Campaigns Against Other Nations

A. By Eli:
   None recorded.
B. By Saul:
   1. Victory over Ammon, which had threatened Jabesh Gilead east of the Jordan (1 Sam. 11).
   2. Victory over the Amalekites in the south (1 Sam. 15:1–9).
   3. Miscellaneous victories over Moab, Edom, and the kings of Zobah, along with mention of previously listed victories over Ammon and Amalek (1 Sam. 14:47–48).
C. By David:
   1. Subdued the Jebusites, from whom he took Jerusalem (2 Sam. 5:6–10).
   2. Subdued Moab (2 Sam. 8:2).
   3. Subdued the Aramaeans
      a. under Hadadezer, king of Zobah (2 Sam. 8:3, 12).
      b. of Damascus (2 Sam. 8:5–6).
      c. of Zoba(h), Beth Rehob, Ish-Tob, and Maacah (2 Sam. 10:8).

4. Subdued Ammon and its Aramaean confederates (2 Sam. 8:12; 10; 12:29–31).
5. Subdued the Edomites (2 Sam. 8:14).
6. Accepted submission of Toi, king of Hamath (perhaps a Hurrian), without force of arms (2 Sam. 8:9–11).

Covenant Leaders

A nation does not live by the sword any more than a person lives by bread alone. A nation's fate often is determined by its leadership. So also this period in the history of Israel is told in terms of its covenant representatives: Eli, Samuel, Saul, and David. Their roles furnish the following outline of the two books of Samuel:

   I. Samuel (1 Sam. 1–7)
     A. Eli and Samuel (chaps. 1–4)
     B. Samuel (chaps. 5–7)
  II. Saul (1 Sam. 8–31)
     A. Saul and Samuel (chaps. 8–15)
     B. Saul and David (chaps. 16–31)
 III. David (2 Sam. 1–24)
     A. Rise to Power (chaps. 1–10)
     B. Fall and Family Strife (chaps. 11–21)
     C. Parting Words and Incidents of Rule (chaps. 22–24)

ELI

Eli, the second-last of the judges, was an old man when he entered the record. There is no indication of what he had accomplished during the 40 years of his judgeship. But the fact that he could function as the high priest at the central sanctuary at Shiloh presupposes some stability within Israel. Though God-fearing and pious, he lacked the aggressiveness and firmness required of an administrator. His judgeship (and life) ended at the news of the death of his undisciplined sons, of the defeat of Israel in battle, and of the loss of the ark to the Philistines. Never had such a disgrace been heaped on Israel! His newborn grandsons's name, Ichabod (literally, "where is glory"), characterized the degrading situation: "The glory has departed from Israel" (1 Sam. 4:19–22).

SAMUEL

The brief chapter of Eli's life seems to serve merely as a means to introduce the most significant person after Moses: Samuel, who may be called "Israel's Second Founder." Although he brought relief to Israel from the Philistine stranglehold, he is not called a military leader but a judge (1 Sam. 7:12–15). Yet Samuel's defeat of the Philistines resulted in enough freedom of movement to permit him regularly to leave his home in Rama(h) and to go "from year to year on a circuit to Bethel, Gilgal, and Mizpah, and [judge] Israel in all those places" (7:16).

Like Moses, he was a prophet (cf. Acts 13:20), for Samuel was first of all Israel's preacher of repentance (1 Sam. 7). As God's spokesman, he also established the monarchy and anointed the first two kings, Saul and David, while guarding the sanctity of Israel's covenant status against royal encroachment, especially by Saul. He did this even after his death when in the dark night before the battle of Gilboa Saul sought Samuel's supernatural support through the witch of Endor (28:4–25).

Samuel died before David became king over Israel (25:1), but his anointing of this shepherd of Bethlehem was an act of faith that was not put to shame.

Samuel's stature in God's drama of salvation is reflected in the Magnificat of Mary (Luke 1:46–55). At the prospect of the birth of the Savior, Mary is constrained to praise the mercy of God in words similar to those in which Hannah, Samuel's mother, had rejoiced in God's deliverance of His people (1 Sam. 2:1–10).

SAUL

Eli and Samuel, like Moses, were descendants of Levi. The first king of Israel was a Benjaminite. Tall, handsome, popular, devout, courageous, resolute, and an open channel for the transmission of charismatic gifts,[10] Saul seems to have had all the necessary qualifications of royalty.

He was appointed to the kingship by three separate and distinct ceremonies at three different places but with one common factor: Samuel as "master of ceremonies."

At the first ceremony, in "the land of Zuph" and at "the outskirts of the city" of Rama(h), Samuel anointed Saul in private to be "commander"[11] over His people (9:27–10:1). Perhaps in order not to overwhelm the peasant Saul, Samuel refrained from calling

---

[10]When "the Spirit of God came upon Saul" (1 Sam. 11:6), he was prompted to muster Israel for battle against the Ammonites. Cf. also 10:6–13; 19:23–24. See also the discussion of "spiritual life" under "Covenant Blessings Under the Monarchy" in this chapter.

[11]The Hebrew word translated "commander" or "prince" (RSV) is used for various positions of authority from heads of families (e.g., 2 Chron. 11:22) to the supreme leadership of all the people (cf. Ezek. 34:24; 37:24).

him the future king but used a more general term. Yet Saul was assured of divine sanction and aid for a totally unexpected position of leadership in Israel. And Saul was given three signs to help him believe that the Lord had chosen him for this undreamed-of role and distinction (10:1–7).

The second ceremony, at Mizpah, sought to persuade the people that God was granting their request for a king and that God had chosen Saul, the son of Kish. This was done through the casting of lots, administered by Samuel (vv. 17–27). Most of the people were convinced of Saul's right to the kingship by this method, although some still repudiated him.

Saul's general acceptance as king took place at still a third convocation, this time at Gilgal. The people called it a "renewing" of the kingdom and sanctified it with peace offerings (11:14–15).[12]

Saul had excellent personal assets and for a time rendered valuable service to his people. Nevertheless, he died a failure, rejected by God. His mistakes may appear trivial and pardonable on the surface, but neither God nor Samuel, His spokesman, acted unjustly in declaring this first king a failure.

First, he did not wait for Samuel to sacrifice before a battle but took on himself the right to officiate (13:5–15). Second, Saul chose to disobey God's command to destroy everything and everybody after a victory over the Amalekites; he spared the king and the best of the booty (chap. 15).

These sins appear as slight peccadillos in comparison to the heinous crimes of later kings, including David's murder and adultery. But no man of clay dare presume to dictate to God how He is to administer either His long-suffering mercy or His punitive justice in the life of an individual or of a whole nation. Any attempt to do so fashions God in the image of one's own idolatrous thinking. This precise sin of dethroning God was the base of Saul's sin. Who was king in Israel, Saul or the Lord of hosts? In his royal person Saul challenged the validity and binding character of God's established order for His people. Israel was a "church"; Saul wanted to make it a "state." Israel was governed by a "constitution"; Saul wanted to be dictator.[13] God did not tolerate such an arrogant challenge to His rulership at this critical juncture, the beginning of the monarchy. Truly, God judges the heart.

---

[12]Because these three acts of "coronation" are interspersed with accounts of other events, the author may have arranged his material in a nonchronological sequence.

[13]The short account of Saul's reign gives other evidence of Saul's arrogant impulsiveness and growing despotic egotism (cf. 1 Sam. 14:24–30; also his sinful treatment of David).

After the Lord had "rejected him from reigning over Israel . . . the Spirit of the Lord departed from Saul, and a distressing spirit[14] from the Lord troubled him" (16:1, 14).

Saul's monarchy did not seriously alter Israel's national structure as a confederacy of tribes. Saul seemingly derived financial support by some taxation (17:25) and took steps toward forming a standing army (14:52). But there is no evidence that he established a bureaucratic chain of command. He built no castle but kept his "royal residence" in his native Gibea. Only a few intimates (including his cousin Abner) constituted his modest court. With these minor adaptions to a monarchy Saul appears to have overcome some initial opposition to his person and to have kept the loyalty of the entire nation (10:27).

Militarily, Saul's reign accomplished little. At his death (hastened by his own hand, 31:4) Israel was again at the mercy of the Philistines, who dominated all of Canaan west of the Jordan River. Ishbosheth, Saul's son, sought safety east of the Jordan and there set up a pretense of rulership.

DAVID

The first book of Samuel had recorded David's anointing by Samuel (16:1–13), his entry into Saul's service (16:14–18:30), and his flight from Saul (chaps. 19–31). The second book, "after the death of Saul," tells of David's rise to power. Because of his significance for covenant history, his life's account receives more space in the Old Testament than that of any other character. A few salient features (in addition to the previous list of battles and victories) should be mentioned.

David was the youngest of eight sons of Jesse. As so often, God chose the person who was least likely to succeed to be the instrument of His might and power. Perhaps 10 years or so elapsed after Samuel had anointed him before he became king of all Israel at the age of 30 (2 Sam. 5:4). These intervening years, filled with high drama and severe testings of faith, included some realistic training for David.

The author selects a number of incidents from this period to set forth (1) God's providential guidance of His protégé and (2) David's willingness to let God choose the road to the throne. (Again, these accounts may not be in chronological order, nor can

---

[14]Because of the lack of detail, Saul's exact mental illness cannot be described in modern psychiatric terms. Scripture says only that he was "troubled," which in Hebrew implies a sudden attack of instability. Efforts to cure it by music proved ineffective.

the exact circumstances surrounding each situation be established.)

Some events[15] appear to be similar, but the differentiating details preclude them from being mere recensions of the same event.

The bulk of 1 Sam. 19–31 reports Saul's persecution of David and the latter's resultant flights for safety to:

1. Rama(h) to be with Samuel at Naioth (19:18–24);
2. a secret meeting with Jonathan (chap. 20);
3. Nob to be with Ahimelech, the priest (21:1–9);
4. Achish, the Philistine king at Gath (21:10–15);
5. the cave of Adullam (22:1–5);
6. the forest of Hereth (22:5);
7. Keilah (23:1–13);
8. the cities of Ziph and En Gedi in the wilderness of Judah (23:14–24, 29);
9. the city of Carmel, where he married Abigail (chap. 25); and
10. the cities of Gath and Ziklag in Philistia (chap. 27; 29:6; 30:26; 2 Sam. 1:1).

After Saul's death the tribe of Judah acclaimed David as king (2 Sam. 2:1–4). When Saul's son Ishbosheth was assassinated by two fellow Benjaminites, and Saul's cousin and army commander Abner (1 Sam. 14:50) was murdered, "all the tribes of Israel came to David at Hebron . . . [where] they anointed David king over Israel" (2 Sam. 5:1, 3). From this time on, his path to power within and without rose steadily.

Governmental functions developed more fully under David than under Saul's initial monarchy, and control was centralized in the person of the king. The list of David's officials for the various functions of state (civil and military) in 2 Sam. 8:15–18 and 20:23–26 indicates a well-developed government operation. For example, David had appointed Joab as commander-in-chief of the army. The chain of command seems to have involved two upper echelons known as the "Three" and the "Thirty." Three distinct army groups apparently formed the nucleus of David's armed forces: a detachment of 600 veterans of David's battles prior to Saul's death, a troop named after the city of Gath and under the command of Ittai, and a bodyguard referred to as "Cherethites [Cretans] and Philistines." Judicial powers were vested in the king

---

[15]E.g., David's coming into the service of Saul (1 Sam. 16:14–17:55) and his sparing of Saul's life on two occasions in the wilderness of Judah (chaps. 24 and 26).

(15:2) and were delegated by him to others. Finances necessary for the maintenance of this host of "servants of the king" and for his standing army were raised by taxation. There was even an official "in charge of the forced labor" (20:24 RSV, NIV—but NKJV: "in charge of revenue").

David appears to have had no difficulty in administering his far-flung empire, but he failed to master himself and to maintain order in his own family. His sin against the sanctity of life and the family (i.e., adultery with Bathsheba and the planned death of her husband, Uriah—chap. 11) touched off a chain reaction of incest, rape, murder, intrigue, and revolution in his own household. His son Absalom's coup and death completely unnerved the king. In his grief (19:4–8) he forgot his duties to the nation, and he made several decisions that showed he had lost the ability to feel instinctively what action was proper and fitting in a given situation. (Cf. the appointment of Amasa to replace Joab and David's treatment of Mephibosheth, Saul's son—19:11–30).

Regardless of the circumstances, royal sin is no less censurable and self-destructive than the wickedness of ordinary people under covenant principles. And the prophet Nathan had the courage to speak the words of indictment to David: "You are the man!"

Though both Saul and David sinned against God and His covenant, the difference between Saul's deep-seated presumption and David's moral lapses must be kept in mind. David repented "out of the depths" (Ps. 130), and pardon was pronounced with divine finality. Heinous and black though his crimes had been, David's submission to theocratic sanctions left him a usable though chastened instrument of God's rule over His people. In contrast to Saul, David showed himself responsive to God's ordinances and did not willfully set aside basic covenant principles to further the power of the crown.

The events and the words of David preserved for us in chapters 21–24 come from various periods of David's reign:

The famine "in the days of David" that prompted the deliverance of seven descendants of Saul to Gibeon for execution (21:1–11).
The burial of the bones of Saul and Jonathan (21:12–14).
Episodes from the Philistine wars (21:15–22).[16]

---

[16]The Hebrew text for 21:19 tells of the slaying of Goliath by one of David's heroes, Elhanan. The NKJV supplies the words "brother of" before the name Goliath on the basis of 1 Chron. 20:5: "Elhanan . . . killed Lahmi the brother of Goliath the Gittite." The text in 1 Chronicles is to be preferred and supplements the reading in 2 Sam. 21:19.

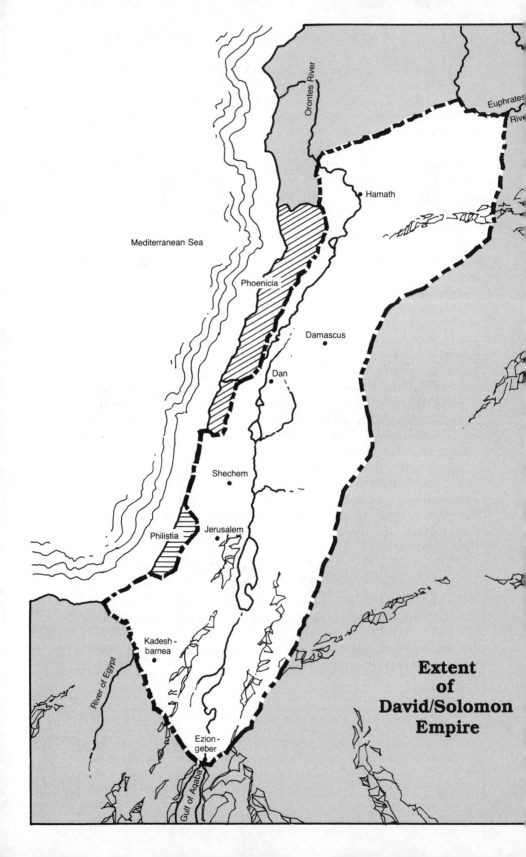

Orontes River

Euphrates River

Hamath

Mediterranean Sea

Phoenicia

Damascus

Dan

Shechem

Philistia

Jerusalem

Kadesh-barnea

River of Egypt

Ezion-geber

Gulf of Aqaba

Extent of David/Solomon Empire

A song of David "on the day when the LORD had delivered him
from the hand of all his enemies, and from the hand of
Saul" (chap. 22; cf. Ps. 18).

"The last words of David" (23:1–7).

A list of "the mighty men whom David had" and some of their
deeds of valor (23:8–39).

David's census of Israel and the punishing pestilence (chap.
24).[17]

• • • • •

David, the Man After God's Heart

In recognition of David, the successors to his throne are eval-
uated on the basis of whether they did "what was right in the
sight of the LORD, according to all that his father David had done"
(2 Kings 18:3; cf. 1 Kings 15:3, 11; 2 Kings 14:3). His loyalty to
God and his importance as God's instrument in promoting His
plan of salvation is thereby fully recognized and normative in spite
of a full knowledge of David's defects and shortcomings. The recognition of David magnifies the grace of God rather than idolizes
the man.

God had endowed David with physical charm, a poetic soul,
a captivating and inspiring personality, and a sure instinct for
choosing the right word and the appropriate action in a given
situation—a combination of leadership qualities rarely found in
one person.

David gave abundant evidence that a God-fearing leader need
not be a blundering fool. He shrewdly exploited each new development for the advancement of his cause. With skill and tact he
knew how to ingratiate himself with friend and foe and how to
heal the divisions in Israel. His choice of neutral Jerusalem as his
capital was a diplomatic triumph. His grief at the death of Saul
and Jonathan was sincere and not a mere "playing to the galler-
ies"; he expressed it, and it won him friends. His treatment of
Saul's offspring was dictated by kindness as well as by prudence.
As pointed out, after the harrowing experience of Absalom's revolt,
David was not his old self. But this human and unflattering account only makes his true greatness shine in even greater glory.

David lives in the record not as a ghost conjured up by a

---

[17]In 2 Samuel the instigation "to number Israel and Judah" proceeds from the
Lord, but in 1 Chron. 21:1 "Satan . . . moved David." Both are true, for in God's
providence Satan is given the role of the tempter of people. The census was reprehensible as an expression of trust in armaments and the monarchy instead of
in the Lord of hosts. But David also in this situation says penitently, "I have sinned,
and I have done wickedly" (24:17).

historian but as a man of flesh and blood—tempted always and at times overcome by lust and pride, yet accepted by God's forgiving mercy and usable for a role of glory unattained after him.

The messianic promise to David and his house (2 Sam. 7) marks an important juncture in covenant revelation. The human ancestry of the Savior, the Mediator of the second covenant, is progressively identified. The large circle of humanity has been narrowed to Shem (Gen. 9:26), of his sons to Abraham (Gen. 12:3), of his offspring to the tribe of Judah (Gen. 49:10), and of this tribe to the house of David. Centuries later Mary, espoused to Joseph the "son of David" (Matt. 1:20), received the final definitive announcement: "You will . . . bring forth a Son . . . and of His kingdom there will be no end" (Luke 1:31, 33).

12. 1 and 2 Kings

THE BOOKS OF SAMUEL AND KINGS COMPARED

In the Septuagint, an ancient Greek translation of the Old Testament, these books are titled "3 and 4 Kings," whereas the two books of Samuel are labeled "1 and 2 Kings." This grouping does not presume to indicate identity of authorship. But it does call attention to the fact that these four volumes record the history of the monarchy in Israel from its origin in 2 Samuel to its ignominious end in 2 Kings. The continuity of this long story is provided by the opening chapters of 1 Kings, which depict the final years of the reign of David, the hero of 2 Samuel.

But the books of Kings differ from the Samuel accounts in several respects. In Samuel the events take place in a time span measured by decades; in Kings they cover nearly four centuries. In Samuel there are three main characters (the person bearing the name of the books and two kings); in Kings the action is restricted to the reign of one person (Solomon) until after his death, when some 40 royal individuals occupy front and center of the scene. About half of them reigned in Israel, the confederation of 10 tribes that seceded from the dynasty of David and lasted about two centuries. During this period, 12 loyal successors of Solomon ruled in Jerusalem. Nine more kings acceded to the throne of David for a little over a century after the fall of Israel. This mélange of leading characters becomes so complex that for a time kings with the same name (Jehoram) held sway in each kingdom.

The books of Kings differ from Samuel also in the way this large number of leading characters is organized into a structured framework. Among the information listed in each case is (1) the time of accession to the throne of the new king in terms of the regnal year of the contemporary monarch in the other kingdom, (2) the age of the king, (3) the length of his reign, and (4) an appraisal of the king's character.

Another feature not found in Samuel but prominent in Kings is the frequent reference to documents containing "the rest of the acts" of a given king. The author had to have access to additional records in reviewing events that occurred over several hundred years. Other authors (e.g., of Judges and Samuel) must have used sources also, but Kings makes more than a passing reference to such compendiums of history. The books of Kings cite them explicitly some 30 times in stereotypic formulas. The reader is directed to supplementary records in each of the divided kingdoms—in the northern part, "the book of the kings of Israel"; in the southern, "the book of the kings of Judah." The content of these noncanonical works is unknown because they are no longer extant. (Nor are those mentioned in Chronicles; cf. 2 Chron. 9:29; 12:15; etc.)

More glaring and crucial than the divergent literary organization of Samuel and Kings is the status of the covenant nation as depicted at the end of each book. In Samuel, an upward movement reaches its culmination in the reign of David, who not only attained full sovereignty and independence for his people but also international fame and imperial recognition. In Kings, a decline soon set in that resulted in deepest degradation and abject humiliation. Because the chosen nation broke the covenant, the holy city and the temple were reduced to ashes, torched by the Babylonian conqueror. The inhabitants of the city and the land were not only reduced to vassalage, but a large number of them were dragged off to the faraway country of the foreign overlord.

Humanly speaking, the people's hopes for survival were as dead as the dry bones in Ezekiel's vision (Ezek. 37). Never again would an earthly descendant of David lay claim to the throne of the covenant nation and rule over it in royal independence. Later confirming this sad state of affairs, the mob reviling Jesus at His trial shouted, "We have no king but Caesar!" (John 19:15), the Herods being but Rome's puppets. In order to mock the servile status of the Jewish people, Pilate put this inscription on the cross of the condemned criminal: "Jesus of Nazareth, the King of the Jews" (v. 19).

In spite of their dreary ending, the books of Kings remain open to the future. The liberation of the Davidic king Jehoiachin, recorded in the last two verses of 2 Kings, may be regarded as a token of the deliverance God had in store for all nations. For, all appearance to the contrary, the Lord of history would not fail to keep His covenant and "the sure mercies of David" (Acts 13:34; Is. 55:3) to raise up "a horn of salvation for us in the house of his servant David" (Luke 1:69). In God's own way and in the fulness of time, a King would ascend "the throne of His father David. . . . Of His kingdom there will be no end" (Luke 1:32–33). Although His kingdom was not of this world, "all nations shall come and worship before" Him, for "He is Lord of lords and King of kings" (Rev. 15:4; 17:14; cf. 19:16).

Although differing in several respects, the books of Samuel and Kings have a basic motif in common, which accounts for their inclusion in that part of the Hebrew canon called the "Former Prophets." Though annalistic in form and content, the books of

Kings sustain the prophetic proclamation, affirming that everything happens according to "the determined counsel and foreknowledge of God" (Acts 2:23). In keeping with this axiom, the record in Kings presents but another chapter in the history of the chosen nation and documents God's faithfulness in keeping His eternal covenant—its blessings as well as its judgments.

Consequently, the author was particular in choosing data to incorporate in his account. From 400 years of Israel's history, he carefully selected the incidents and situations that bear witness to God's direction of the course of history in order to "remember His holy covenant" (Luke 1:72).

The author's eclectic procedure is evident also in his discriminating use of the sources at his disposal, "the acts of the kings of Israel and Judah." Thus he accords to King Jeroboam of Israel only seven verses, though this monarch reigned for 41 years (2 Kings 14:23–29). For the same reason, the author compresses into 18 verses the report of King Manasseh of Judah, whose wicked rule lasted 55 years (21:1–18). Furthermore, it is indicative of the kind of history the author set out to furnish that about one-third of its pages are devoted to telling the stories of two ancient messengers of God's covenant: Elijah and Elisha, the contemporary kings being little more than a foil for their prophetic activity (1 Kings 17–22; 2 Kings 1–9).

AUTHORSHIP

The author of 1 and 2 Kings is unknown. The same holds true of the other books in the collection of the "Former Prophets." Jeremiah has been suggested as filling the role, but that is unlikely. He was carried off to Egypt and did not witness the release of Jehoiachin from prison in Babylonia some time later. At any rate, anonymity of a Biblical book does not detract from its inspired character or authority.

NOTES ON CHRONOLOGY

The books of Kings use an intricately synchronized system of chronology. Scores of events in each kingdom are dated in relation to fixed points of time in the other kingdom as well as in the reigns of foreign rulers. In order to demonstrate that these numbers of years are consistent with one another in specific instances and in their totals one must first establish the prevailing systems of dating on which the figures are based. Once the different methods of computing regnal years (methods used in the author's sources) have been discovered, most of the apparent inconsistencies disappear. One should be aware also that in the transmission of so many dates some errors could have slipped into our Hebrew manuscripts.

Of course, no dates in the text are given according to a fixed point in modern chronology, that is "in such-and-such a year B.C." Nevertheless, taking into account all possibilities, events have been tagged with dates of present-day reckoning. So for example, it has long been agreed that the fall of Israel occurred in 722 B.C., and that of Judah in 587/6 B.C.

The Kings of the Divided Kingdom (931—586 B.C.)

Judah	Israel	
	, Period of Mutual Hostilities	
Rehoboam	Jeroboam I	
Abijah		
Asa	Nadab	
	Baasha	
	Elah	
	Zimri (7 days)	
	Omri	
	Period of Peaceful Relations	
	Ahab	Ahab slain shortly after the Battle of Qarqar, 853 B.C., against Assyrian Shalmaneser III.
Jehoshaphat		
	Ahaziah	
	J(eh)oram	
Jehoram		
	Period of Renewed Hostilities	
Ahaziah (1 year)	Jehu	
Athaliah		
Joash		
	Jehoahaz	
	J(eh)oash	
Amaziah		
	Jeroboam II	
Uzziah/ Azariah		

	Zachariah	
	(6 months)	
	Shallum	
	(1 month)	
	Menahem	
		Tiglath-Pileser III of Assyria collects tribute from Azariah and Menahem, 742/741 B.C.
Jotham		
	Pekahiah	
	Pekah	
Ahaz		
	Hoshea	
Hezekiah		
	Fall of Samaria, 722 B.C., by Shalmaneser V, who died same year.	
		Assyrian General Sennacherib invades Judah, 701 B.C.
Manasseh		
Amon		
Josiah		Josiah killed by Egyptian Pharaoh Necho, 609 B.C.
Jehoahaz		
(3 months)		
Jehoiakim		
Jehoiachin		Jehoiachin captured by Nebuchadnezzar, 597 B.C.
(3 months)		
Zedekiah		
Fall of Jerusalem, 586 B.C., to Nebuchadnezzar		

A History of the Covenant People and Its Kings: From Heights of Glory to Depths of Degradation

THE FOUNDING OF THE DAVIDIC DYNASTY (1 KINGS 1–2)

Continuing the account of David's reign supplied in 1 and 2 Samuel, the opening chapters of 1 Kings record how this great king relinquished the throne to a coregent[1] and successor: Solomon. Though feeble and drained of physical vitality, David was able to rouse himself to resolute and drastic action in making his and Bathsheba's son his royal heir. Thereby he founded a dynasty

---

[1]Coregencies no doubt occurred also in later regimes. One is explicitly mentioned in the case of King Azariah and his son Jotham (2 Kings 15:5).

that was to endure for four centuries. (How long Solomon exercised royal functions during the remaining years of David's lifetime is not said.)

Before the old king died, he also formally admonished his son to "keep the charge of the LORD your God: to walk in His ways" as set forth in the covenant (1 Kings 2:3). Although he observed this directive only imperfectly in his reign, Solomon promptly obeyed his father's specific order to eliminate those guilty of challenging his accession to the throne and to execute the culprits.

SOLOMON'S REIGN (1 KINGS 3–11)

Solomon ruled the covenant nation for 40 years, a period of internal and external tranquility as well as unprecedented prosperity and grandeur.

Solomon's Personal Traits and Administrative Acumen (Chapters 3–4)

The account of Solomon's reign opens and closes with a candid appraisal of his character and conduct. To his credit it is noted that the basic desire of his heart (he "loved the LORD") prompted him to walk "in the statutes of his father David" (3:3).

This unequivocal affirmation of a noble motivation in Solomon's life is not retracted, but the sacred writer does not gloss over or minimize this king's lapses into failures to obey divinely prescribed precepts. No excuse is offered for his flouting the sacred ordinances of worship as he "sacrificed and burned incense at the high place" (v. 3). Himself guilty of engaging in unlawful ceremonial rites, he also tolerated it when "the people sacrificed at the high places" (v. 2).

Just as glaring was his violation of the law governing his marital status. Disregarding the prohibition against foreign wives, he married an Egyptian princess and also added "many foreign women" to his harem. The result of this grandiose lifestyle was so disastrous that when he was old, "his wives turned his heart after other gods" (11:4).

Admittedly far from perfect in his personal life, Solomon did evince his desire to love the Lord and to please Him by the way he sought to discharge responsibilities as head of state. When the Lord appeared to him at the beginning of his reign and in a dream promised Solomon whatever he desired, the young king acknowledged that he owed the accession to the throne solely to divine goodness and providence (3:4–6). Declining a gift of material benefits, he asked to be granted the ability to "discern between good and evil" in the administration of his office (v. 9). He would not establish his own criterion of right and wrong but would act in accordance with a divine gift of "an understanding heart"— literally a "listening heart"—attuned and obedient to God's will.

Solomon's claim to the throne met with popular approval. When David gave him his own mule to ride from nearby Gibeon into Jerusalem, the people acclaimed him by shouting: "Long live King Solomon!" (1:32–39). When in the fullness of time One "greater than Solomon" (Matt. 12:42) chose the same kind of animal to bear Him from Bethphage to the Holy City, the attendant multitudes no doubt recalled the ancient coronation scenario and expressed their hope for the coming of a mighty earthly ruler and deliverer by crying out: "Hosanna to the Son of David!" (Matt. 21:1–11).

Finally, "the kingdom was established in the hand of Solomon" (1 King 2:46) when the high priest Zadok "took a horn of oil from the tabernacle and anointed Solomon" (1:39).

Solomon, Builder and Royal Executive (Chapters 5–11)

The most momentous achievement of his reign was the building of an edifice of wood and stone where God, whom "heaven and the heaven of heavens cannot contain" (8:27), condescended to "dwell" for the covenant people and where He promised to receive their worship and to hear their prayers. In order to forestall false notions of His presence, Solomon stressed repeatedly in his dedicatory prayer (8:22–61) that "the Most High" cannot be impounded in temples made with hands (Acts 7:48) to be manipulated by magic and incantations. For when the people would "pray toward this place" (1 Kings 8:30), they were to know that God's power to forgive and deliver them was not restricted to the confines of a local shrine, but He would "hear in heaven [His] dwelling place" (v. 39), transcending the world He created.

The building materials of the temple were supplied by Hiram, king of Tyre (5:1–11). When they arrived at the site, the materials were prepared and fitted into place by a large group of laborers conscripted by royal decree and directed by a contingent of supervisors (vv. 13–18).

Though much data of the temple's dimension is provided (chap. 6), it does not recreate an architect's blueprint of all its features. Nevertheless, it is possible to reconstruct a plan of its overall size and design.

The temple proper was a rectangular structure open to the east. If the Biblical cubit measured 18 inches, it was 90 feet long, 30 feet wide, and 45 feet high. At its western end stood "the inner sanctuary," "the Most Holy Place." A cube of 30 feet, it contained the Ark of the Covenant and was entered only by the high priest on the Day of Atonement. The remaining 60-foot length made up the nave, or "Holy Place," to which only the priests had access. Around these sacred premises, also on their western side, was a subsidiary structure. Built into the walls of the main edifice and reaching a height of only 27 feet, it contained "side chambers" that possibly served as storage chambers and/or living quarters for the priests.

Extending eastward from the nave stood a "vestibule" or "porch" (7:15–22). A flight of steps led up to it, and on either side stood two huge columns known as "Jachin" and "Boaz."

Interspersed in the description of the temple (chaps. 6–7) are reports of its furnishings. Some of these are described in detail, such as the Ark of the Covenant and its attendant cherubim, the table of showbread, the lampstand, and the lavers or wash basins. The utensils used by the priests were of gold. Lavish use of the precious metal was also made in overlaying the wooden walls and floors.

Besides the temple, Solomon engaged in other extensive building enterprises. Among the edifices he erected were his own house, the "House of the Forest of Lebanon," and a house for Pharaoh's daughter. He also improved the fortification of Jerusalem and built several cities to make the borders of the land secure against invasion.

To pay for his costly building program and to provide payment for his sumptuous court, Solomon introduced several unpopular administrative innovations. Ignoring the traditional boundaries of the tribes, he divided the land into 12 districts for taxation purposes (4:7). Each governor of his area was required to supply the funds necessary to maintain the royal household for a month. Even more galling was Solomon's decree instituting a conscripted labor force (5:13).

These repressive measures aroused his subjects to an intense resentment of his reign. An attempted revolt shattered the long-prevailing peace. Ringleaders of the uprising eluded apprehension and were given asylum in Egypt. One of them, Jeroboam, returned to his home base after the death of Solomon and was able to have himself made king of the 10 northern tribes, thus dividing the nation into two hostile camps (chap. 12).

This tragic schism did not happen by chance. It was the Lord's scourge on a disobedient king and on a people who followed that king's example of paying homage to the false gods of the neighboring heathen nations. Already before the division God had warned through His messenger: "I will tear the kingdom out of the hand of Solomon" (11:31). And He did.

THE DIVIDED KINGDOM (1 KINGS 12–2 KINGS 25)

As foretold by the Lord, the disruption of Solomon's kingdom became a reality when his son Rehoboam refused to rescind the obnoxious policies of his father (12:15). Embittered by the prospect of continued oppression, the 10 northern tribes, hereafter called "Israel," seceded from the union and elected as king a man who had been Solomon's "officer over all the labor force" in their area (11:28). The remaining southern kingdom was known as "Judah" because it consisted largely of that tribe.

The rift in the covenant nation was never to be healed. Politically, it was a disastrous turning point in the history of both kingdoms.

Disaster for Israel: Israel lost its independence and vanished from the scene after about two centuries (930–722 B.C.). Conceived and born in strife and dissension, this coalition of insurgents, though larger in territory and richer in resources than its southern rival, lacked sustained stability in government. During its existence of a little more than 200 years, no less than 19 kings claimed the throne. Because no recognized system of regnal succession was in effect, as many as nine dynastic changes occurred, almost all in the wake of assassinations and regicides.

Nevertheless, several of Israel's rulers distinguished themselves in astute statecraft and successful military operations. Engaged periodically in conflict with belligerent Judah, the northern kings were able to hold their own. At one point, one of them (Baasha) even pressured his southern contemporary (Asa) until he pleaded for foreign aid to ward off Baasha's invasion forces (15:16–20).

Except for an interlude of about 30 years, the relationship between the two kingdoms from beginning to end remained hostile.

In the area of religion, the division of Solomon's empire resulted in flagrant covenant aberrations. The first king of northern Israel, in order to dissuade his subjects from participating in the temple services in Jerusalem, the capital of the southern kingdom, introduced what at best amounted to a syncretistic form of worship. At Bethel and Dan, cities on the southern and northern boundaries of his domain, Jeroboam erected a calf or bullock overlaid with gold in flagrant violation of covenant law, which forbade making a graven image of the Lord. Of this manufactured deity he blatantly proclaimed: "Here are your gods, O Israel, which brought you up from the land of Egypt!" (12:28). Because his successors perpetuated this idolatrous worship, they too were charged with "the sins of Jeroboam, which he had sinned and by

The Divided Kingdoms

Sea of Galilee

ISRAEL

Samaria

Jerusalem

Dead Sea

JUDAH

which he had made Israel sin" (15:30; cf. v. 34; 16:2).

The Lord, long patient and forbearing, finally put an end to these abominations. Executing God's wrath on the apostate people, the Assyrian king (Shalmaneser) in 722 B.C., captured and destroyed Samaria, the northern kingdom's capital city, carried off into exile a major portion of the population (2 Kings 17:1–6), and colonized the conquered territory with his own subjects (v. 24). The indigenous survivors of the conquest lost not only their identity but also their allegiance to the true religion by intermarriage with the imported idolatrous settlers (vv. 33–41). As a result, the Jews even at Jesus' time had "no dealings with Samaritans" (John 4:9).

Disaster for Judah: The division of the kingdom also affected Judah adversely, though it survived Israel by more than a century (722–586 B.C.). Its territory, bordering its rival only a few miles north of Jerusalem, faced the desert to the south and lacked access to the trade routes and commercial enterprises.

Offsetting these handicaps was the benefit of the traditions associated with the holy city of Jerusalem and the temple of Solomon. Another asset consisted in the unbroken succession of its kings. While Israel was wracked by frequent and violent dynastic changes, Judah's line of descent from the house and lineage of David remained intact. This stabilizing factor accounts for the fact that, whereas as many as 19 kings ruled in Israel for 200 years, the same number of Davidic descendants (plus a queen) held sway for over 300 years.

By the grace of God Judah survived Israel's eclipse by more than a century. But some of Judah's kings also incurred the wrath of the Lord by tolerating and even promoting the worship of idolatrous abominations. Serving as the instrument of divine judgment, the Babylonian king Nebuchadnezzar ravished the Judean countryside, destroyed Jerusalem together with its temple, and in 587 B.C. carried off into exile a good portion of the subjugated population (2 Kings 24–25).

What led to the tragic end of both segments of the covenant nation is told by the sacred historian beginning with 1 Kings 12. Pursuing that purpose, he records pertinent events as they transpired during the reigns of individual kings of Israel and Judah. But he also insists that the factor determining the course of events is not the ingenuity and administrative skill of the occupants of the throne, but whether they did evil or good in the sight of the Lord.

A Period[2] of Mutual Hostility (1 Kings 12–16)

It began almost at once after the division of Solomon's kingdom. The latter's son and successor, Rehoboam, tried to engage in a military campaign against Jeroboam, the rebel king, to bring the seceding tribes back into the union. Though he was forbidden by the Lord to attack his northern kinsmen, tension and animosity did not subside; the sacred writer notes that "there was war between Rehoboam and Jeroboam all their days" (14:30). As mentioned above, Asa, the third successor of Solomon, did not hesitate to invoke military aid from a foreign power against his northern rival.

Not seriously affected by external pressure, northern Israel was wracked by civil strife soon after Jeroboam's death. His son barely began to reign when he was assassinated—as were three other contenders for the throne. A captain of the cavalry, Omri, eventually seized the reigns of government. He restored order for the remainder of this period, made the city of Samaria his capital, and achieved international acclaim. The author of Kings nevertheless devoted only eight verses to describe his regime (16:21–28).

During Omri's latter days and those of Asa of Judah, the hostility between the rival kingdom subsided and gave way to a conciliatory spirit. After their deaths, hostilities ended for a while.

A Period of Peaceful Relations (1 Kings 16–2 Kings 8)

This period was initiated officially when Asa's son "made peace with the king of Israel" (1 Kings 22:44). The resulting rapprochement not only ended the era of mutual antagonism but also provided so firm a bond of cooperation that the former rivals undertook joint military action against a foreign enemy. In fact, a permanent union of the two kingdoms seemed possible when the two royal families intermarried. The merger was consummated when Athaliah, the daughter of Israel's wicked king Ahab and his equally infamous queen, Jezebel, became the wife of Judah's king, Jehoram.

During the short time of political peace, the religious conditions were in a state of unprecedented turmoil and confusion, particularly during the reign of Ahab and Jezebel, the "Lady Macbeth" of the Old Testament. They not only abetted and fostered the prevailing apostasy but even sought to suppress loyalty to

---

[2]Significant in the history of the divided kingdom is the changing relationship of the two regimes to one another. Because it seriously affected the course of events, it affords a division of this era into epochs.

God's covenant. To counteract these abominations, the Lord raised up the prophets Elijah and Elisha. What these mighty defenders and protagonists of the true faith did and endured is recorded at great length by the sacred historian (but will be reviewed in a subsequent part of this survey).

A lasting healing of ruptured relationships, however, did not materialize. All hopes of its success vanished when Jehu, a captain in Israel's army, killed both his own king and the occupant of Judah's throne. As a result, their successors resumed mutual hostilities.

A Period of Renewed Strife (2 Kings 9–17)

An overt clash between the two regimes was precipitated when the Judean king Ahaziah foolishly dared his contemporary in Israel, "Come, let us face one another in battle" (14:8). The southern challenger was not only defeated, but the victor even invaded Judah, broke down the wall of Jerusalem, robbed the king's house and the house of the Lord of its treasures, and took hostages (vv. 8–14). Apparently he did not take advantage of his successes to continue the conflict.

Soon after this incident, the people of both kingdoms enjoyed a season of unprecedented prosperity. The greed and unscrupulous business tactics that it spawned resulted in heartless oppression and extortion of the poor. These rampant covenant violations were vehemently denounced in Israel by the prophets Amos and Hosea and in Judah by Micah and Isaiah. While their messages and careers are not incorporated in the annals of Kings, these messengers of God affirm and condemn the same social evils in both kingdoms.

The king of Israel who supplied the circumstances favorable to profitable commercial enterprises and the rise of a wealthy class bore the same name as the first ruler of the divided kingdom. To distinguish him from his namesake, he has been designated Jeroboam II. Acceding to the throne after the divided kingdom had existed about a century and a half, he was the fourth in an unbroken line of kings founded by Jehu, who, as already noted, ended the era of peace between the rival kingdoms by slaying his predecessor as well as the king of Judah and his progeny.

But after Jeroboam II, the Jehu dynasty of five kings came to an end and gave way to bloody rivalry. Jeroboam's son was murdered, and his assassin in turn met the same fate. The reign of the next three kings was cut short by regicides. Even Hoshea (not the prophet but the last of Israel's kings) seized control by killing his royal predecessor.

By this time the Lord of history had at hand a foreign nation capable of executing judgment on His people who had rebelled against Him for so long. Unconsciously doing God's will, Tiglath-Pileser, the king of a revived Assyria, subjugated large areas of Israelite territory and carried their inhabitants "captive to Assyria" (15:29). When King Hoshea later withheld tribute from the next king of Assyria, Shalmaneser, the rebellious vassal was shut up and bound in prison (17:4). But the vengeance of Shalmaneser did not abate until he had captured Samaria, and "Israel was carried away from their own land to Assyria" (v. 23).

By the grace and forbearance of God, the southern kingdom was not destroyed by the Assyrian conqueror, though "also Judah did not keep the commandments of the LORD their God, but walked in the statutes of Israel which they made" (17:19). Judah was also spared the internal instability caused by frequent dynastic change that plagued Israel. But at one point the lineage of David almost became extinct when Athaliah, the mother of the just-slain Judean king Ahaziah (8:25–26) and daughter of Ahab and Jezebel, seized the throne (11:1). Bereft of her own children, she sought to consolidate her reign—and the house of Ahab over Judah—by killing all the royal seed of David. The sole survivor of this massacre was an infant named Joash, Ahaziah's son and Athaliah's grandson. Together with his nurse, he was hidden from his grandmother by his aunt (his father's sister) in her bedroom and then in the temple for six years. In his seventh year, the wicked queen was slain in a coup d'état led by the high priest, and Joash was declared king in her stead, thus preserving the Davidic succession of kings (11:1–16).

But this internal strife was soon to be overshadowed by a threat to the independence of all citizens of Judah as hostilities between the two kingdoms flared up again during the reign of King Ahaz of Judah, the fourth successor of Joash. At that time, King Pekah of Israel allied himself with a Syrian ruler and besieged Jerusalem (16:5). Though in dire straits, Ahaz refused to believe the promise of divine deliverance conveyed to him by the prophet Isaiah[3] and instead "sent messengers to Tiglath-Pileser king of Assyria, saying 'I am your servant and your son. Come up and save me from the hand of the king of Syria and from the hand of the king of Israel' " (16:7). Responding to this abject plea for help, the king of Assyria invaded Syria and captured Damascus, its capital. As a result, the siege of Jerusalem had to be abandoned.

But the Assyrian lust for power was not sated by its conquests

---

[3]See Is. 7 for the Immanuel prophecy delivered to Ahaz during this so-called Syro-Ephraimitic War.

on the northern perimeter of Israel. Only 10 years later the successor of Tiglath-Pileser captured Samaria and drove the inhabitants of the northern kingdom into exile (17:1–7). This happened in the fourth year of Hezekiah, who presumably exercised the royal function in Judah as the coregent of his father, Ahaz. Hezekiah also had to become a tribute-paying vassal of the Assyrian invader. What happened when "he rebelled against the king of Assyria" (18:7) will be reviewed in the next section.

The Last Kings of Judah (2 Kings 18–25)

In the 14th year of Hezekiah, King Sennacherib of Assyria was able to embark on a punitive foray against his rebellious vassal and took "all the fortified cities of Judah" (18:13). Not satisfied with Hezekiah's submission and the payment of a huge amount of tribute, the incensed conqueror threatened to capture and destroy Jerusalem, blasphemously defying the Lord to deliver the city from his hand (vv. 17–35). Disregarding this proud boast, Hezekiah turned to the Lord in prayer for help. "And it came to pass on a certain night that the angel of the LORD went out, and killed in the camp of the Assyrians one hundred and eighty-five thousand" (19:35). His army destroyed, Sennacherib "departed . . . and remained at Nineveh," where his two sons "struck him down with the sword" (vv. 36–37). (For a parallel account of this episode, see Is. 36–37).

But the time was to come when the Lord would "also remove Judah from My sight" (2 Kings 23:27). Meanwhile, the rod of His anger was no longer the Assyrian world power but its successor in the Tigris-Euphrates Valley, the Babylonian empire. When its founder firmly controlled his home base, he relied on his son Nebuchadnezzar to extend his dominion over adjacent territories, including the land of Judah. In doing so, General Nebuchadnezzar had to meet and overcome the expansionist designs of the Egyptian Pharaoh Necho to incorporate the same area in his domain.

To meet and confront his Babylonian rival, Necho proceeded up the Mediterranean coastal plain. When he reached Megiddo at its northern end, Judean King Josiah tried to stop him but was defeated and killed in the ensuing battle (23:29). Resuming his march northward, Necho conquered the territory of the Syrians and set up temporary headquarters at Riblah, a city north of Damascus on the main highway from Egypt to the Euphrates. Here he held court to assert his full grip on vanquished Judah. Ordering Josiah's successor, Jehoahaz, to appear before him, Necho deposed him, sent him bound to Egypt, and replaced him with his brother, Eliakim. To impress on the latter that he ruled only by the grace of the Pharaoh, Necho changed Eliakim's name to

Jehoiakim and imposed a huge tribute of gold and silver (23:33–34).

But Judah was soon to exchange Egyptian for Babylonian vassalage (24:7). For when Necho met his Babylonian challenger at Carchemish on the headwaters of the Euphrates, he was soundly defeated. Nebuchadnezzar pursued his erstwhile rival over the route Necho had come all the way to the border of Egypt. Helpless against the victorious invader, neighboring Judah acknowledged Nebuchadnezzar's supremacy, and Jehoiakim became his servant (v. 1).

Now the stage was set for the last acts and the denouement in the drama played by the kings of the covenant nation. Scene after scene followed in an unbroken sequence of disasters.

The first in the series of events to precipitate the tragedy occurred when, after only three years, Jehoiakim rebelled against his Babylonian overlord, who now had become *King* Nebuchadnezzar. After a short delay, the latter was able to deal with the uprising. But by the time his army invaded and besieged Jerusalem, Jehoiakim had died. His 18-year-old successor, Jehoiachin, was forced to surrender (v. 12) and was imprisoned in Babylon for 37 years (25:27). Carried off into captivity with him were thousands of the upper stratum of the population (24:14).

"Then the king of Babylon made Mattaniah, Jehoiachin's uncle, king in his place, and changed his name to Zedekiah" (v. 17). He too "rebelled against the king of Babylon" (v. 20). After a prolonged siege, the army of the Chaldean king (his dynastic title) "burned the house of the Lord, . . . broke down the walls of Jerusalem all around, . . . [and] carried away captive the rest of the people, . . . [leaving only] the poor of the land as vinedressers and farmers" (25:9–12).

Zedekiah tried to escape but was captured and brought before Nebuchadnezzar at Riblah, where Necho previously held court. "Then they killed the sons of Zedekiah before his eyes, put out the eyes of Zedekiah, bound him with bronze fetters, and took him to Babylon" (v. 7).

To administer the area he had added to his conquests, Nebuchadnezzar appointed as his governor a man named Gedaliah. But fanatics of "the royal family" killed him and his associates, both "the Jews, and the Chaldeans who were with him." Fearing retribution for their senseless act, they fled to Egypt (vv. 22–26).

On the surface it might appear that the destruction of Jerusalem resulted from the superior military forces of its enemies. But the true cause of its downfall was rebellion against the Lord, which aroused "the fierceness of His great wrath . . . against Judah" and provoked Him to declare, "I will also remove Judah from

My sight, as I have removed Israel, and will cast off this city Jerusalem which I have chosen, and the house of which I said, 'My name shall be there' " (23:26–27).

But not all the seven kings of this era were guilty of doing evil in the sight of the Lord. The first who "trusted in the LORD . . . [and] kept His commandments, which the LORD had commanded Moses" (18:5–6) was Hezekiah. "He removed the high places and broke the sacred pillars, cut down the wooden images and broke in pieces the bronze serpent that Moses had made; for until those days the children of Israel burned incense to it" (v. 4).

About a half-century later, Josiah also "did what was right in the sight of the LORD" (22:2). To promote the worship of the true God, he ordered the repair of the temple. In the accumulated debris a book was found (evidently Deuteronomy), for he could read "all the words of the Book of the Covenant" before the assembly of all the people (23:2). In obedience to its content, he "made a covenant before the LORD . . . to perform the words of this covenant that were written in this book" (v. 3) and reinstituted the celebration of the Passover prescribed in Deut. 16 (2 Kings 23:21–22). He also destroyed "all the articles that were made for Baal" found in the temple, as well as those scattered throughout his realm (vv. 4–20). Because he would thus humble himself before the Lord, Huldah the prophetess had assured him that the calamity about to befall Jerusalem would be deferred until after he had died (22:19–20).

Unfortunately, the reforms introduced by each of these two pious kings lasted only during their reigns. Their successors again departed from the Lord and provoked Him to execute judgment on the apostate nation.

Hezekiah's reform had as one of its worst offenders Manasseh, Hezekiah's own son and immediate successor. Ignoring the deliverance of his father by the angel of the Lord (19:35) and the miracles done in his behalf (chap. 20), Manasseh introduced and promoted "the abominations of the nations whom the LORD had cast out before the children of Israel" (21:2). During his long reign of 55 years he not only "made Judah sin with his idols" (v. 11) but also shed "very much innocent blood" (v. 16) of those who refused to obey his directives. Outraged by this monster of iniquity who "acted more wickedly than all the Amorites who were before him" (v. 10), the Lord reiterated His threat: "I will forsake the remnant of My inheritance and deliver them into the hand of their enemies" (v. 14).

The covenant made by Josiah likewise was broken after his death. His three successors, including the last king, Zedekiah, provoked the Lord to execute His fierce wrath, for each of them again "did evil in the sight of the LORD" (21:22; 23:37; 24:9, 19).

Divine Messengers of the Covenant

The Lord did not fail to instruct the covenant people in the way of righteousness and to warn them of the consequences of disobedience to His holy will. For He "testified against Israel and against Judah, by all His prophets, namely every seer, saying, 'Turn from your evil ways, and keep My commandments and My statutes' " (2 Kings 17:13).

Some of them remained unidentified and are called only "a man of God" or "a prophet" (see, e.g., 1 Kings 13:1, 20). Others are supplied with names but without additional information regarding their persons, as for example, Ahijah the Shilonite and Jehu the son of Hanani (11:29; 16:7). It may seem strange that no mention is made of well-known divine emissaries who also were active during the same time and have filled whole books with the word of God spoken by them, such as Amos, Hosea, and Micah. Since the inspired author's purpose was to furnish a history of Israel and Judah ruled by kings, he apparently restricted himself to report only the careers of the prophets who made contact with the contemporary occupants of the throne and played a part in directing events during their reigns. Accordingly, the sacred chronicler mentions the prophet Nathan, active in David's struggle to make Solomon his successor. Reference is also made to Isaiah because he delivered God's word to King Hezekiah. But the activities of two other prophets are reported at far greater length.

ELIJAH (1 KINGS 17–21; 2 KINGS 2:1–12)

The principal target of his ministry was the wicked King Ahab. Appearing before him as if from nowhere (17:1), Elijah announced the coming of a severe drought. When it arrived, the Lord supplied His prophet with drink from the Brook Cherith and with food brought to him by ravens. Because the brook also dried up, the Lord ordered Elijah to seek refuge beyond the reach of Ahab in Zarephath, a city in the territory of Phoenician Sidon. Here Elijah provided a miraculous supply of flour and oil for the widow who had fed him. And when her son became sick and died, Elijah was granted the power to revive the young boy.

After three years Elijah obeyed the command of the Lord to appear again before Ahab and to announce the end of the drought (18:1). On this occasion he demonstrated to the king and an assembly of people that the Lord controlled the forces of nature and was the true God of Israel. For in answer to Elijah's prayer, fire rained from heaven and devoured his altar and the sacrifice on it, all thoroughly drenched with water. The prophets of Baal, challenged to prove that their god could do likewise, had already failed miserably, taunted and ridiculed by Elijah. Proved to be impostors, they were seized by the people and executed by the prophet of the Lord.

Elijah now faced the wrath of Ahab's wicked wife, Jezebel. Unnerved by her threat to kill him (19:2), as she had already done to other faithful prophets, he fled the land of Israel and sought safety in Beersheba on the southern border of Judah. From there he proceeded farther south to Mount Horeb (Mount Sinai; v. 8), sustained on his journey of 40 days and nights by food that an angel had provided for him at the outset. Here where Moses had met with the Lord, the runaway prophet was given to hear "a still small voice" (v. 12) to impress on him that he was to resume his ministry motivated by a quiet appeal to his inner self rather than by the dramatic display of God's power over nature that had taken place earlier.

Reinstated as the Lord's emissary, Elijah again confronted Ahab in Samaria (21:17–29) to denounce him for illegally confiscating the vineyard of Naboth, the hereditary owner, after Jezebel had arranged his execution on trumped-up charges of blasphemy. Of Jezebel the prophet announced that "the dogs shall eat Jezebel by the wall of Jezreel" (v. 23). The king repented of his misdeed and was granted a reprieve from the punishment awaiting him (v. 29).

Elijah also transmitted the word of the Lord to Ahab's successor, Ahaziah (2 Kings 1:2–4). The latter sent messengers to Baal-Zebub, the god of Ekron, to inquire whether their master would recover from an injury sustained when he fell from an upper room. Prompted by God, Elijah met them on their way and sent word back to the king informing him that he would die. Ahaziah twice sent a captain with 50 men to capture Elijah, but each time they were consumed by fire from heaven. At Ahaziah's third try, the angel of the Lord told Elijah to go to Ahaziah and personally repeat that the king would " 'not come down from the bed to which you have gone up, but you shall surely die.' So Ahaziah died according to the word of the LORD" (vv. 16–17).

The end of Elijah's career came at Jericho across the Jordan (2:1–12). There "suddenly a chariot of fire appeared with horses of fire, . . . and Elijah went up by a whirlwind into heaven" (v.

11).[4] Before his spectacular departure and at God's direction he had chosen Elisha as his successor, his associate and understudy.

ELISHA (1 KINGS 19:16, 19—21; 2 KINGS 2—9; 13:14—20)

Still a young man when he was endowed with a double portion of Elijah's spirit at the latter's translation from this earth (2 Kings 2), Elisha served as the Lord's prophet to five successors of Ahab, a period of some 50 years. Like his "father" and mentor, Elijah's successor gave evidence of his divine mission by being enabled by the Spirit of God to prophesy while in a state of ecstasy (3:14—15). By the power of the same Spirit he also performed supernatural feats and wonders.[5] Most of them were done to vindicate himself as the Lord's anointed. In some instances, they resembled acts recorded of Elijah.

Elisha also directed the course of national and international events. At the beginning of his ministry, he carried out the divine directive, previously assigned to Elijah (1 Kings 19:15), to anoint Hazael as king of Syria (2 Kings 8:1—13) and Jehu as king of Israel (9:1—10). At another time he cured Naaman, a commander of the King of Syria, of his leprosy by ordering him to wash seven times in the Jordan (5:1—14).

Even after Elisha's death, his corpse gave evidence of the power that the Lord had granted him during his lifetime. For when his lifeless body came into contact with the mortal remains of a soldier thrown into the same grave, the latter was restored to life (13:14—21).

• • • • •

Epilog

The account of the books of Kings, from the glory of Solomon's reign to the enslavement of the covenant people, bears witness to the fact that no matter at what cost, "God is not mocked" (Gal. 6:7).

At the same time the subsequent history reveals no less clearly that the Lord's "mercy is everlasting, and His truth endures to all generations" (Ps. 100:5; cf. Ps. 30:5). For in spite of human frailty and infidelity, He kept His promise to bless all nations through Abraham and his seed so that eventually "salvation is of the Jews" (John 4:22).

---

[4]For Elijah's appearance together with Moses at the transfiguration of Jesus, see Matt. 17:3.

[5]E.g., 2 Kings 2:14, 19—22; 4:1—7, 18—36, 38—41, 42—44; 6:1—7, 8—17, 18—20.

To implement His gracious purpose through His people, the Lord of the nations in due time summoned another power to act as His servant. According to the books of Ezra and Nehemiah, the king of Persia released the chastened chosen people from bondage and permitted them to return to the Promised Land. From the midst of the land and the people and from the "lineage of David" (Luke 2:4) there was to come "a Savior, who is Christ the Lord" (v. 11).

13. 1 and 2 Chronicles

The books preceding Chronicles present a continuous historical progression from creation and the age of the patriarchs to the formation of the chosen people (Gen.–Deut.), from Israel's occupation of the Promised Land to the turbulent period of the judges (Joshua–Ruth), and from David's and Solomon's days of glory to the fall of Jerusalem and the Babylonian captivity (Sam.–Kings).

Surprisingly, the two books of Chronicles[1] traverse the same millennia as Genesis to Kings. The story begins again with Adam and ends at a point only a quarter-century after the last event in 2 Kings: the liberation of Jehoiachin, king of Judah, from a Babylonian prison in 562 B.C. (2 Kings 25:29). Second Chronicles 36:22–23 adds that when the Persian king Cyrus became the new world ruler in 538 B.C., he issued a decree of general amnesty, permitting the exiles[2] to return to their homeland.

But this review of bygone ages is not simply a condensation of history from Genesis to Kings nor even a balanced resume of Israel's past. Although some accounts here have a counterpart in Samuel and Kings, Chronicles is not designed to recapitulate the contents of those books.

As one obvious indication of the special interest of Chronicles, note the large number of pages allotted to some phases of history in comparison with others. Of its 65 chapters, almost one-third (19) are taken up with the account of a single individual, David (1 Chron. 11–29). By contrast, the eons preceding his reign are compressed into introductory genealogical lists comprising only nine chapters (1 Chron. 1–9). The same amount is devoted to the activities of another individual, David's son Solomon (2 Chron. 1–9). The 400 years of the divided kingdom are covered in just 27 chapters (2 Chron. 10–36).

As further indication of its special interest, Chronicles not only assigns a disproportionate amount of space to David and Solomon (almost half of its pages), but it also restricts its reports

---

[1]In the Hebrew Bible, these two books have the title "Words [relating events] of the Days." The English name "Chronicles" derives from the Latin word *chronicum*, a term that Jerome, translator of the Vulgate, applied to them. He states that they constitute "a *chronicum* [a book of annals] of the entire divine history."

[2]Although a list of people "who dwelt again in their homeland" appears in 1 Chron. 9, and a list of the royal descendants of David in 1 Chron. 3:10–24, no postexilic events are mentioned in Chronicles.

on these two kings almost entirely to a single aspect of their reigns. The focus is not their political achievements (which receive only passing attention) or their personal lives (which go practically unnoticed). Rather, interest centers in what these men did at the pinnacle of Israel's outward glory to further the spiritual edification of their people. Chronicles contains extensive and detailed reports on how these men planned, built, and dedicated the temple; how they promoted true worship forms; how they fostered music as a prominent feature of the services; how they were careful to have only authorized personnel officiate in the temple.

There is a reason that these special interests loom so large in this survey spanning millennia: Chronicles, written after the exile, had something to say *from the past* to people who recently and barely had survived extinction in the land of their Babylonian captors. Even though the people again walked the soil of their fathers, they could not blink away the humiliating fact that they were "servants" of the Persian king (Neh. 9:36–37). Prospects of becoming "a light to the Gentiles" (Is. 49:6; cf. Luke 2:32) appeared to lie buried in the ruins of the temple and in the rubble of the holy city.

To this dispirited band of immigrants, Chronicles recalled history from the perspective of God's "everlasting covenant" with David—"the sure mercies of David" (Is. 55:3). To those who lamented, "Our hope is lost" (Ezek. 37:11), the reminder of God's "steadfast sure love for David" proclaimed, "There is hope in your future" (Jer. 31:17). So, for example, each name in the lists of ancient forebears (1 Chron. 1–9) was not just the bare statistical entry of an archivist. The genealogies going back to Adam were a sustained litany, intoned so persistently as to bring every doubting heart in tune with its message: "All appearances to the contrary, you are the people whom the Creator of all people has chosen in order to bless all the families of the earth" (cf. Gen. 12:1–3).

For the same reason, Chronicles lets Israel's past glory shine into its dark days of the postexilic period. To a people who now owed a precarious existence to the grace of a foreign ruler, the past sang out: "What these leaders of Israel achieved shows that the Lord of history truly is able to let His kingdom come according to His determinate counsel and will. Nations rise and fall at His command."

But Chronicles reviews history in its unique way for another reason. Although "in great distress and reproach" (Neh. 1:3) and in need of encouragement, the nation needed instruction in righteousness. The chosen people were to learn from the past also that they had no future if they obstinately "sinned against Your [God's] judgments, which if a man does, he shall live by them" (9:29).

The cardinal sin was idolatry. It canceled all covenant promises and invoked dire curses. On the other hand, undivided devotion of the heart was to be expressed through rites prescribed by God, by officiants appointed by Him, and in the place designated by Him. Therefore, the temple, once planned by David and built by Solomon but now in ruins, spoke of what had been and again must be central in the relationship of Israel to God. The temple and its proper worship were the heartbeat of the nation; here grace and mercy sustained its life.

By the same token, Israel's history showed that its downfall began when it no longer worshiped God according to His ordinances. Its neglect of prescribed forms of worship was the outward symptom of an internal malady. The neglect proved that the people did not love the Lord with all their heart and with all their soul and with all their strength (Deut. 6:5). Ritual disobedience proved to be a spring from which flowed all the other foul waters of covenant disloyalty, including the sins against the neighbor.

AUTHORSHIP

Scripture nowhere identifies the author of Chronicles. Jewish tradition suggests that Ezra wrote it. Many modern scholars hold that it forms a trilogy with the books of Ezra and Nehemiah, all three being composed by an anonymous writer called "the Chronicler." In any case, the contents of Chronicles do not require a date of composition later than the last quarter of the fifth century B.C.

Sources

There are more references to sources in Chronicles than in any other Old Testament book. Covering eons of past history, the author was dependent on records for most of his material.

For the five centuries from Saul to the exile, the author mentions a large variety of documents to which he was indebted for his data (e.g., "in the book of Samuel the seer, in the book of Nathan the prophet, and in the book of Gad the seer"—1 Chron. 29:29). No doubt he was acquainted with the canonical books of Samuel and Kings, which span the same period. But for much of his material, he went back to the same sources used for these Biblical books (cf., e.g., 1 Kings 14:19, 29 with 2 Chron. 24:27).

For the detailed genealogies of the first nine chapters and elsewhere, the writer must have had access to statistical records in addition to the genealogical tables preserved in the canonical books.

Historically Trustworthy

Many students of the Bible have found it hard to believe that Chronicles presents accurate history because of the numbers recorded there. Although in most instances they are in full agreement with those found in Samuel-Kings, there are two areas in which the numbers cause difficulty: (1) Some of them diverge from the numbers in Samuel-Kings,[3] and (2) some seem too large to be possible. A few examples of each are cited here to illustrate the problem.

Differences

1.	1 Chron. 21:12 — three years	2 Sam. 24:13 — seven
2.	2 Chron. 2:2 — 3,600 overseers	1 Kings 5:16 — 3,300
3.	2 Chron. 3:15 — 35 cubits	1 Kings 7:15 — 18
4.	2 Chron. 4:5 — 3,000 "baths"	1 Kings 7:26 — 2,000
5.	2 Chron. 8:18 — 450 gold talents	1 Kings 9:28 — 420

Larger Numbers[4]

1.	2 Chron. 3:4 — 120 cubits	1 Kings 6:2 — 30
2.	1 Chron. 18:4 — 7,000 horsemen	2 Sam. 8:4 — 700
3.	1 Chron. 19:18 — 7,000 chariots	2 Sam. 10:18 — 700

Some of these apparent discrepancies may have resulted from mistakes made by ancient copyists of texts. This possibility of error is enhanced in view of the fact that ancient writers did not have modern Arabic numerals at their disposal. It appears that at some time letters of the alphabet were used to signify numbers, letters that could easily have been misread. There is also good reason to believe that a numerical notation in vogue consisted of horizontal and vertical strokes, another source of error.

Although these factors may dispose of some of the problems of computation encountered in Chronicles, Biblical research at present lacks an adequate explanation for every instance. But there is reason to hope that continued textual and archaeological studies will make it possible to understand what the numerical notations in Chronicles actually mean. At the same time, there is no reason to believe that the chronicler deliberately falsified the account to embellish and glorify the history of the covenant nation.

---

[3]Not all ancient versions of a given Bible passage contain the same number, and not all English Bible translations use the same ancient manuscripts. Therefore, while discrepancies may appear in one translation, they might not appear in another.

[4]In some cases a smaller number is given in Chronicles than in Samuel-Kings. For example, 2 Chron. 9:25 — 4,000 stalls; 1 Kings 4:26 — 40,000.

The Contents

The contents of the books may be roughly divided into four parts:

1. The genealogies (1 Chron. 1–9)
2. The reign of David (1 Chron. 10–29)
3. The reign of Solomon (2 Chron. 1–9)
4. The kings of Judah until the exile (2 Chron. 10–36)

THE GENEALOGIES (1 CHRONICLES 1–9)

Israel's ancestral history begins with Adam in order to place God's people into its proper setting among the peoples of the earth. This nation was but one of many nations of the earth yet was chosen by God to be a special nation (chap. 1).

The 12 tribes are listed according to a double order: the order of birth of the sons of Jacob (briefly noted in 2:1–2) and the order in which the tribes settled the land.

A. In the main list, the families of **Judah** stand first (2:1–4:23), given special prominence because his line included David, Solomon, and their royal sons (chap. 3).

B. The tribe of **Simeon** (4:24–43) was small and had only a few large families. Some of them emigrated to other places in and around Canaan and settled land that had belonged to the foreign nations. A few of these families still lived there at the time of the writer.

C. **Reuben** (5:1–10), the firstborn, who had lost his birthright to Joseph, was also a small tribe and lived on the east side of the Jordan. But it was rich and powerful by the time of Saul.

D. **Gad** (5:11–22) was situated just north of Reuben.

E. **Half of Manasseh** (5:23–26), a large group, lived north of both Gad and Reuben.

F. The three sons of **Levi** (chap. 6) did not have any territory but received cities for their own from the lands of the other tribes. The genealogy singles out the sons of Aaron, who became the priests, and the sons of Kohath and Merari, who served and sang in the temple.

G. The other tribes, **Issachar, Benjamin, Naphtali, Ephraim,** and **Asher** are listed briefly (chap. 7). The sons of Benjamin are listed a second time (chap. 8) to show the genealogy of King Saul and his family.

Chapter 9 lists the main people who came back from the exile in Babylon and "dwelt in their possessions" (v. 2). The priests and

Levites who returned receive the longest listing.

This chapter ends (vv. 35–44) with a repetition of part of the genealogy of Saul as a transition to the next section, which begins with the death of Saul and the rise of David.

THE REIGN OF DAVID (1 CHRONICLES 10–29)

As a true man of God, David carried out the command that had been given to Joshua but had never been completely fulfilled: to take the whole land from the nations who inhabited it. It was to reach from the river of Egypt (a desert river south of Judah) to the Euphrates. Under David, the land of Israel reached these dimensions.[5] He achieved this in obedience to God's command— but only with fierce warfare. Because David had "shed much blood," God did not allow him to build the temple (22:7–10). Yet David was allowed to render service to the institution of Israel's worship. He wrested Jerusalem (11:4–8) from the Jebusites (whom Joshua had never conquered) and made that city the capital of the nation. He brought the long-neglected Ark of the Covenant to Jerusalem and centralized public worship there (chap. 15). And although the Lord told him that he could not build a temple, David was still concerned that it should be built. He drew up plans for the temple at the Lord's direction (22:1–7; 28:10–12, 19) so that his son could build it.

When David was old, he assembled the leaders of Israel in order to:

1. organize the Levites and assign them their functions (chaps. 23–26);
2. organize the government and army under rulers and generals (chap. 27); and
3. name Solomon to follow Him on the throne (chaps. 28–29).

Before David died, he gave Solomon final instructions to build the temple and turned over to him both the plans and all the funds that he had collected for the task (28:11–19).

THE REIGN OF SOLOMON (2 CHRONICLES 1–9)

After Solomon was established on the throne, the Lord appeared to him in a vision and let him ask for the desires of his heart. When Solomon asked only for wisdom and knowledge to

---

[5]For some reason, David never conquered Phoenicia but maintained friendly relations with it. Solomon did the same and received assistance from that country in building the temple.

rule the people well, the Lord granted him also riches and honor that would be the envy of the world (chap. 1). And indeed, gold and silver were said to become as common as stones in Jerusalem (1:15; 9:27).

In building the temple, Solomon wrote to Hiram, king of Tyre (Phoenicia), for assistance (2:3–10). Because of the friendly relations that had existed between David and Hiram, the latter agreed to send men and materials. Solomon gathered 150,000 aliens from the land of Israel to do the heavy work (2:17–18).

The temple was built with all the elegance and beauty available. It was constructed after the general pattern of the tabernacle with a vestibule, a court, the Holy Place, and the Most Holy Place (chap. 3). The furnishings and equipment were made mainly of gold and the walls of cypress wood (chap. 4). In addition, the gold, the silver, and the vessels that David had dedicated were stored in the temple (5:1).

When the building was finished, Solomon assembled all the leaders of Israel (chap. 5) to bring the old tabernacle with all its furnishings up to the temple—especially the Ark of the Covenant to be placed in the Most Holy Place. There was music and praise, and the glory of the Lord filled the temple.

Solomon's long dedicatory prayer (6:12–42) recalled the promise of God to David that his son should build the temple and sit on the throne, and his sons after him forever. Solomon acknowledged that the temple could not contain God, who dwells in heaven, but he prayed that the Lord would hear the prayers addressed to Him in this house where God had set His name. He besought God to judge and protect Israel, to forgive sin, to shed His glory abroad, and to give victory to Israel.

When Solomon had finished praying, fire from heaven consumed the offerings (7:1). So many sacrifices were offered that day that the altar could not hold them all. After the two-week celebration (vv. 8–9), the Lord appeared to Solomon in a vision at night (vv. 12–22) and told him that his prayer would be answered and that He would hear the prayers of Israel spoken in the temple whenever they would be offered in true repentance. God also renewed the promise He had made to David that He would never "fail to have a man as ruler in Israel" (v. 18).

In addition to erecting the temple, Solomon built cities (8:4–6), exacting forced labor from the aliens in the land (vv. 7–10). He moved his wife, an Egyptian princess, into her own house, no doubt because she was a pagan (v. 11). He also reestablished the divisions of priests, Levites, and gatekeepers in accordance with the commands of David, and he offered the sacrifices on the festival days (vv. 12–15).

Under the peacetime reign of Solomon, great wealth and pomp flowed into Jerusalem, so much that even the visiting queen of Sheba had to see it to believe it (chap. 9) and was astonished.

THE KINGS OF JUDAH UNTIL THE EXILE (2 CHRONICLES 10–36)

After the death of Solomon, his son **Rehoboam** became king. **Jeroboam,** with the older royal advisors, asked him to lighten the yoke (of taxes) that Solomon had imposed on Israel to build the temples and palaces in Jerusalem. Rehoboam did not take the advice of the elders but followed his young advisors, who urged that he increase the burdens. All of Israel except for Judah and Benjamin forsook Rehoboam and thereafter remained in rebellion until obliterated by Assyria (chap. 10). Rehoboam did not try to force the northern tribes back into subjection but instead built up the fortunes and fortresses of Judah (11:2–17).

When Rehoboam died, **Abijah,** his son, reigned (13:1). Jeroboam (still king of the northern tribes) made war against Abijah (perhaps hoping to reunite the two kingdoms under himself). But because Abijah relied on the Lord, he won out in spite of two-to-one odds.

When he died, his son **Asa** ruled in his place. Asa also was a good king at first, and under him Judah prospered and was victorious—even defeating an Egyptian army of about a million men (14:9–15). At the words of the prophet Azariah, Asa repaired the temple and removed many of the idols that had become numerous in the land. He even removed his mother from her station because she was an idolatress (15:16). But Asa failed to abolish all the high places of idolatry. And when Baasha of Israel later threatened Judah (chap. 16), Asa used the temple treasury to buy the military assistance of Syria. The prophet Hanani reproved Asa for not relying on the Lord for strength, and as a result, Asa had wars until he died.

Jehoshaphat was king after him. He was also a good king at first and fostered learning of the Scriptures in Judah. But when Syria threatened Canaan, Jehoshaphat allied himself with northern King Ahab (instead of with the Lord of hosts) to do battle (chap. 18). The war ended when Ahab died (as had been prophesied). But because of his alliance with Ahab, Jehoshaphat incurred the anger of the Lord, who sent some of the surrounding nations to attack Judah. Yet because all Judah and the king himself then called on the Lord, He delivered Judah.

Jehoram, an evil king, ruled after Jehoshaphat. He murdered all his brothers and committed other evils, even setting up high places for the worship of strange gods. As a result, he lost control of Edom, was invaded by the Arabs and Philistines (who carried off almost his entire family), and died in agony.

His son **Ahaziah,** who replaced him, was as evil as his father. After only a year, he was murdered by Jehu of Israel.

Ahaziah's mother, **Athaliah,** ruled for six years and tried to assassinate all heirs to the crown. But Ahaziah's youngest son, Joash, was saved by his aunt. The priests finally put him on the throne and had Athaliah slain (22:10–23:21).

Joash, another good king, restored the temple after collecting a tax on all Judah. But later, when the high priest died, the people turned to their idols, and the Syrians came and looted them. Joash was killed by his own servants.

Amaziah ruled next—also a good king at first (even though he murdered the servants who had executed his father). But eventually he too turned away from the Lord, with the result that Israel defeated him and looted the temple.

The throne then passed to **Uzziah.** He was a good and a powerful king but took it on himself to offer incense in the temple. His haughtiness earned him leprosy, of which he died.

His son **Jotham** restored the temple and subdued the Ammonites.

When he died, **Ahaz** took the throne. This idolater, threatened by several enemies, called for help from the king of Assyria, who only afflicted Ahaz more. Ahaz, "increasingly unfaithful to the LORD" (28:22), closed the temple and set up idols throughout Jerusalem.

When Ahaz died, **Hezekiah,** a good king, reopened the temple (29:3), sanctified it, and restored the sacrifices, the Levitical orders, and the temple treasury. He also ordered the long-neglected Passover to be observed. When King Sennacharib of Assyria came to attack him, the angel of the Lord killed the best of the enemy army, forcing Sennacharib to return home (32:1–21).

Manasseh reigned next and undid everything that his father, Hezekiah, had done. But in his later years, Manasseh repented, restored the temple, and removed the idols from it.

Amon, his evil son, was was killed by his servants.

Eight-year-old **Josiah** then began to reign (34:1). He zealously restored the worship of Judah and destroyed the idols. In the course of the work on the temple, the Book of the Law was found (v. 14) and read, and Josiah and all Judah repented of their sins, kept the Passover, and offered sacrifices. Josiah was killed in battle with the Egyptians, to the grief of all Judah.

After him reigned **Jehoahaz, Jehoiakim,** and **Jehoiachin.** None of these kings stopped the idolatry in Judah; they even encouraged its growth. God's patience had run out (36:16), and Judah was taken into captivity by Babylon.

Zedekiah was placed on the throne for a few years. But when he revolted against Babylon, King Nebuchadnezzar completely destroyed Jerusalem with its temple, carried off Zedekiah and his family and the treasures of the temple to Babylonia, and made Judah a province (vv. 11–21).

• • • • •

Epilog (2 Chronicles 36:22–23)

In spite of Israel's unfaithfulness to the covenant, God, ever merciful and gracious, continued to make the descendants of Abraham His instrument to bless and redeem all nations. He kept His promise, spoken "by the mouth of Jeremiah" (v. 22), saying, "After seventy years are completed at Babylon, I will visit you and perform My good word toward you, and cause you to return to this place" (Jer. 29:10). And so it was that "the LORD stirred up the spirit of Cyrus king of Persia" (2 Chron. 36:22), heir of the Babylonian empire, to release the enslaved people of God and to aid them in resettling the Land of Promise.

This second exodus from captivity is described in the books of Ezra and Nehemiah.

14. Ezra and Nehemiah

The books of Ezra and Nehemiah record how the Babylonian captivity, the tomb of Israel's national identity, became the womb of its rebirth.

The people "from whom, according to the flesh," the Christ was to come (Rom. 9:5) was God's special creation from the beginning. From Abraham, "already dead (since he was about a hundred years old), and the deadness of Sarah's womb" (4:19) would come the Son of promise, "born according to the Spirit" (Gal. 4:29). But soon the offspring of the patriarchs, shut up in the dungeon of Egyptian slavery, seemed destined for oblivion.

Then God spoke His mighty "let My people go" (Ex. 5:1), and a young nation, "a kingdom of priests and a holy nation," (19:6) sprang into being. But the nation turned out to be a disobedient son, unfaithful to its high calling. When the end came, its capital and temple lay in ruins, its land scorched and occupied by the enemy.

With its population decimated and carried into exile, Israel seemed destined to share the fate of all vanquished peoples of antiquity. In the normal course of events, it would have been doomed to extinction in Babylonia, the victim of attrition and absorption by the conqueror.

But God once more spoke a life-giving word, and there was a resurrection of Israel's "dry bones" (Ezek. 37:1–14). There was a second exodus, as foretold by the prophets. And in the Promised Land once more, the seed of Abraham continued to be the people by whom the Lord of the nations was to bless "all the families of the earth" (Gen. 12:3).

There are two phases in the story of Israel's rehabilitation after Babylon. Though reported in separate books, each stage consists of a construction program in wood and stone followed by a reestablishment of moral and spiritual foundations. Ezra records the building of the temple (Ezra 1–6), Nehemiah the erection of Jerusalem's walls (Neh. 1–7). Ezra the priest alone initiates the first spiritual reform (Ezra 7–10); in the second he has the support and collaboration of Nehemiah (Neh. 8:1–13:3), a layman who also takes action independently (13:4–31).

OVERVIEW

The drama of Israel's restoration opens 60 years before Ezra appears on the scene. In 536 B.C., when Jerusalem had been in ruins for half a century, a large contingent of exiles returned to the homeland. Prominent figures in that early period included the two governors, Sheshbazzar and Zerubbabel, and the high priest, Jeshua (Ezra 1:8; 2:2). In their second year the people were ready to begin rebuilding the temple (3:8), but it took 20 difficult years before the returnees were able to complete it in 515 B.C.

The next recorded events are Ezra's return to Jerusalem almost 60 years later (458 B.C.) and his vigorous campaign against mixed marriages, "for Ezra had prepared his heart to seek the Law of the LORD, and to do it, and to teach statutes and ordinances in Israel" (7:10).

After another interval of 12 years, Nehemiah received permission from the Persian king to investigate reports that the repatriated exiles were "in great distress and reproach" (Neh. 1:3). On his arrival in Jerusalem (445 B.C.), he at once set to work to make the city safe against attacks from the outside. Overcoming serious difficulties, he built the walls of the city, organized watchmen to guard them, and persuaded the people to repopulate the city enclosed by the walls. In the spiritual rearmament of the people that followed, he yielded initiative to Ezra.

Apparently recalled by the king, Nehemiah left Jerusalem in 433 B.C. When later he returned, he found it necessary again to correct abuses that had crept in during his absence.

Ezra and Nehemiah, their contributions to Israel's reconstruction made, both vanish from sight as abruptly as they appear on stage.

DURATION OF EZRA-NEHEMIAH

Israel's rehabilitation in the Promised Land as reported in these books did not materialize overnight. The dates in the above résumé make clear that more than 100 years elapsed between the arrival in Jerusalem of the first exiles (536 B.C.) and the reforms carried out by Nehemiah on his second visit to the city (433 B.C.). This century coincided almost exactly with the first half of the duration of the gigantic Persian empire that stretched from the Indus River through Asia Minor to the Mediterranean Sea and down through Palestine to the waters of the Nile. Its turn to be buried under the sands of time would come a hundred years later when in 331 B.C. Alexander the Great would become the next world conqueror.

In both books events are dated according to the regnal years of the following Persian rulers:

Cyrus 539–530	Zerubbabel and Jeshua return to Jerusalem
Cambyses 530–522 (not mentioned)	Rebuilding halted
Darius 522–486	Temple completed 516
Xerxes/Ahasuerus 486–464	(Events in Esther)
Artaxerxes 464–423	Return of Ezra (458) and Nehemiah (445)

Five more kings held the throne in the next century, including another Xerxes, two Dariuses, and two Artaxerxes.

Daniel (a contemporary in part with Cyrus) and Esther (a contemporary of Xerxes) both lived at the time of Ezra and Nehemiah but are not mentioned because they were not involved in the reconstruction program in the homeland.

AUTHORSHIP

Scripture does not make direct statements on the final authorship of these books. According to a widely held theory, they form a literary unit with Chronicles, produced by an unknown person and therefore conveniently called "the Chronicler."[1] There are enough similarities in the three books to suggest that they are the composition of the same writer. Also, a date for one author a century later is advanced because of the inclusion of the genealogy of the high priestly line in Neh. 12:1–11.

But other factors favor individual authorship. Rabbinic tradition, counting Ezra-Nehemiah as one book, holds that "Ezra wrote his book" but adds significantly that Nehemiah "finished it." If true, the first-person accounts in both books are not memoirs incorporated by a compiler but separate autobiographical notes by Ezra and Nehemiah themselves. Both writers present statistical materials based on documents current at their own time. And only Ezra contains sections written in Aramaic (Ezra 4:8–6:18; 7:12–26), at that time the language of international diplomacy.

The Contents
Outline

Rebirth of a Nation

I. Israel's Revival—First Phase (Ezra)
  A. Rebuilding the Temple (chaps. 1–6)

---

[1]Some propose Ezra as the author of the trilogy.

REBUILDING PROJECTS IN EZRA AND NEHEMIAH

(The following discussion does not follow the outline as such, but looks first at the physical rebuilding projects by Ezra and Nehemiah and then at the moral and spiritual rehabilitation under both leaders.)

The Temple (Ezra 1–6)

Ezra 1–2 sets the stage for events culminating in the reconstruction of the temple. In the first year of the repatriation of God's elect in the Promised Land, those who had availed themselves of Cyrus's decree (1:2–4) formed a registered community (chap. 2). After an altar had been erected under the leadership of Jeshua and Zerubbabel (3:2), and after the appointed feasts of the Lord had resumed (vv. 2–6), and after construction workers were hired, then was "laid the foundation of the temple of the LORD [while] according to the ordinance of David king of Israel . . . [the priests and Levites] sang responsively, praising and giving thanks to the Lord" (vv. 10–11).

Unfortunately the completion of the temple was delayed by opposition from the local people of the land, who became "the adversaries of Judah and Benjamin" (4:1). When their proposal to cooperate in the project was refused, they "hired counselors against [the Jews] to frustrate their purpose all the days of Cyrus king of Persia, even until the reign of Darius" (v. 5).

The same adversaries also objected to the building of the walls of Jerusalem during the later reign of Xerxes/Ahasuerus (vv. 6–23). The account of how this obstacle was eventually overcome is inserted here to testify that all building operations by the covenant people succeeded in spite of attempts to stop them.

Returning to the account of the interruption of building the temple, Ezra reports, "Thus the work of the house of God . . . ceased, and it was discontinued until the second year of the reign of Darius" (4:24). How this Persian king reaffirmed the decree, originally issued by Cyrus, to "build the house of the LORD God . . . which is in Jerusalem" (1:3) is told in chapters 5–6. "So the elders of the Jews . . . built and finished [the temple] . . . in the sixth year of the reign of King Darius" (6:14–15).

The Walls of Jerusalem (Nehemiah 1–7)

Supplementing the book of Ezra, Nehemiah also tells of a material reconstruction: the fortification of Jerusalem (chaps. 1–7). The walls of the holy city on ancient foundations rose under the leadership of a highly resourceful and deeply religious layman who held high office at the Persian court. Hearing there of "the great distress and reproach" (1:3) of defenseless Jerusalem and invoking divine blessing on his decision to help (vv. 5–11), Nehemiah requested and received permission from the king to take charge personally of his proposal to rebuild Jerusalem (2:5).

His arrival in Jerusalem for that purpose incensed Persian officials in adjacent areas (vv. 9–10). Aware of their opposition, he secretly surveyed the "broken down" city wall (vv. 11–16) and "its gates which were burned with fire" (v. 13) before he revealed his intentions even to his compatriots (vv. 17–20). Within a short time construction operations were under way (chap. 3). Overcoming machinations by hostile neighbors (chap. 4), dissension in his own ranks (chap. 5), and even attempts on his life (6:1–14), Nehemiah completed the project in a crash program and could report, "So the wall was finished . . . in fifty-two days" (6:15).

Nehemiah also realized that if the completed walls were to make life in the city safe, it would be necessary (1) that they be staffed by enough guards with the gates remaining open only in full daylight (7:1–3) and (2) that the population of the city be increased in order to raise the number of potential defenders (v. 4; 11:1–2). But those who were to be moved into the city from the countryside were to be screened carefully lest subversive elements destroy the city from within. Nehemiah was about to take a census to determine "by genealogy" who the bona fide members in "the province" were, when he came upon "a register of the genealogy of those who had come up [out of exile] in the first return" (7:5), namely at the time when Cyrus issued the decree about 90 years earlier, authorizing the Jews to return to their homeland. This roster of registered families (vv. 6–72) was considered so vital for the future welfare of the city that it was made a part of the record, duplicating the list in Ezra 2. (The report of the repopulation itself is deferred to chap. 11.)

MORAL AND SPIRITUAL REHABILITATION

Mixed Marriages Dissolved (Ezra 9–10)

"In the seventh year of King Artaxerxes" (7:7) Ezra received permission to return to Jerusalem. The king gave him an official letter, authorizing him to (1) visit Jerusalem accompanied by

other volunteers and deliver various donations "for the service of
the house of your God" (vv. 12–20); (2) draw on provincial trea-
suries for money and materials (vv. 21–24); and (3) effect con-
formity to God's Law by appointing judges and magistrates (vv.
25–26).

Arriving in Jerusalem a half century after the temple of wood
and stone had been erected, Ezra realized that a rebuilding of
moral integrity also was essential if the rehabilitation of the covenant people was not to end in national dissolution. He therefore
attacked the existing malady at its roots: the intermarriage of the
chosen people with foreigners (chaps. 9–10). How Ezra went about
convincing the assembled people to put away their "pagan wives"
is told in chapter 10.

Ezra and various leaders (vv. 16–17) prepared a list of those
who, according to Mal. 2:11, had "married the daughter of a foreign god" (Ezra 10:18–44). There were 17 priests, 10 Levites, and
86 laymen—a total of 113 men. In comparison with the total population, this number may not appear alarming. But the danger
of assimilation by the peoples of the land was real in view of the
fact that the clergy and "the leaders and rulers [have] been foremost in this trespass" (9:2). When even "the sons of Jeshua" (high
priest at the time) had set the fashion, the whole populace could
be expected to follow their example of disobedience (10:18). As it
was, repeated efforts were necessary to eradicate the evil (cf. Neh.
13:23–29).

Spiritual Rededication (Nehemiah 8–10)

Nehemiah, the lay governor at the time, yielded to "Ezra the
priest" (cf. Neh. 12:26) in promoting the spiritual rehabilitation
of the people and in committing themselves to a renewal of the
covenant of the Lord.

When "the people gathered together as one man in the open
square [of the city], . . . Ezra the scribe" read to them from "the
Book of the Law of Moses" (8:1). The assembly responded to the
exhortation to comply cheerfully with it (vv. 9–10) by celebrating
the feast of tabernacles "according to the prescribed manner" (vv.
16–18).

A second assembly, at which the congregation appeared "with
fasting, in sackcloth, and with dust on their heads" (9:1), cul-
minated in a formal renewal of the covenant drawn up in an official
document (vv. 5–38). A list of those who ratified the agreement,
headed by Nehemiah, was put on record in 10:1–27. "The rest of
the people" gave a solemn oath "to observe and do all the commandments of the LORD" (vv. 28–39). And the first thing they

pledged was not to "give our daughters as wives to the peoples of the land, nor take their daughters for our sons" (v. 30).

Measures to Promote Rehabilitation (Nehemiah 11–13)

The last three chapters of Nehemiah record additional measures that under this layman's leadership contributed to the rehabilitation of postexilic Israel. Some provided physical security; others strengthened the moral and spiritual life. Some were introduced during his first visit to Jerusalem (11:1–13:3); others on a return to the city some years later (13:4–31). Thus he "cleansed them of everything pagan" (v. 30), and the covenant nation continued to serve as God's instrument in His plan to bless all nations.

• • • • •

In Memoriam

Both Ezra and Nehemiah dropped from sight as suddenly as they appeared on the scene of action. Their full life's story is known only to God. Yet what they did to promote the kingdom of God is a matter of record, "written for our admonition, on whom the ends of the ages have come" (1 Cor. 10:11). He has inscribed their names in the Book of Life, making them citizens of "the great city, the holy Jerusalem," which John saw "descending out of heaven from God" (Rev. 21:9).

15. Esther

INTRODUCTION

The book of Esther does not pick up the thread of history where the two preceding books left it but supplements the record of the same century of postexilic Israel spanned by Ezra and Nehemiah. It tells of events that happened after the rebuilding of the temple (515 B.C.; Ezra 1–6) but before Ezra's arrival in Jerusalem (458 B.C.; Ezra 7–10). But it does not furnish a continuous chronicle of this half-century. The account is limited to a dramatic episode during the early part of the reign of Ahasuerus, or Xerxes (486–464 B.C.), referred to only in passing in Ezra 4:6.

Esther complements Ezra-Nehemiah also as far as the place of action is concerned. The scene shifts from the newly established community in Jerusalem to provinces within the Persian empire where many Jews chose to remain rather than return to the homeland. The court of Xerxes is the focus of attention.

Esther 1–3 introduces the chief actors of a drama full of suspense and sudden reversals. The first to appear on the stage is the Persian king. The fate of the Jews, threatened with extinction, is subject to the whims of this all-powerful ruler (chap. 1). Esther, who became his queen, is the heroine; her cousin and guardian, Mordecai, is the hero (chap. 2). The villain is Xerxes' grand vizier, Haman. The rest of the book plays out the drama to a happy conclusion.

Esther and Ezra-Nehemiah also complement one another most strikingly by their respective portrayals of divine providence. In the latter books, all that happens is ascribed directly to God's action. He "stirred up the spirit of Cyrus" (Ezra 1:1); His "good hand" was on Nehemiah (Neh. 2:8). Ezra's review of history mentions no part played by the great men in Israel's past; they were but channels through whom God governed the universe (Neh. 9:6–37).

Esther seems to go to the other extreme with only one vague reference to divine providence. Even God goes unmentioned throughout the book except for a veiled allusion (4:14: "Deliverance will arise for the Jews from another place"). In this scheme of things, people do not express their dependence on Him. There is no prayer for help when disaster threatens; there is no song of thanksgiving when deliverance comes; there is only action—as if everything depended on human courage and resourcefulness. Concern about this feature of the book was so strong at a later time that apocryphal additions to Esther were composed in which lengthy prayers are placed on the lips of Mordecai and Esther, and the deliverance of the Jews is repeatedly attributed to God.

But even without these apocryphal additions, God's guiding hand is clearly present in the book. Despite their noblest efforts, hero and heroine would have gone down to defeat had it not been that favorable circumstances made success possible. At crucial points, coincidences beyond their control converged to produce situations that spelled the difference between life and death. Similarly, for example, Joseph had seen the same power create the "chance happenings" that determined his life. In both cases, it was not a blind, capricious force but a force that "in all things" deliberately let God "work together for good to those" for whom it shaped events (Rom. 8:28). This force could not be stymied by forces of evil, even if they represented the resources of a world empire. It established a universal tribunal of justice where right and wrong have their day in court. This often unnamed power is "the finger of God" (Ex. 8:19; Luke 11:20).

To those tempted to misunderstand the workings of God's providence, the book of Esther affirms with the New Testament "it is written again" (Matt. 4:7) that He expects people to work out their own salvation even though He bestows it. He lets people reap the fruits of their labor even though He makes them grow. He lets people rejoice in their accomplishments even though their actions are not always blameless.

Authorship

The writer remains unknown. Only general information about him can be gleaned from the book. He composed it sometime after the death of Xerxes (464 B.C.) because he refers to the king's biography, "written in the book of the chronicles of the kings of Media and Persia" (10:2). He also had access to the records kept by Mordecai (9:20, 32). At the same time he draws on his personal acquaintance with Persian life to put events into their proper setting. His incidental descriptions of the palace in Susa (NKJV: Shushan), the royal court (e.g., 1:6–7), and its protocol and customs have been found to be so accurate as to suggest that he was a contemporary of the events he records. A person intimately acquainted with the details is not apt to commit blunders in major historical references (as charged by many scholars). From the opening "now it came to pass" (1:1) to the closing reference to documentation (10:2) he purports to write what actually happened, not a fanciful historical novel.

The Book's Place in the Canon

In our English Bible Esther is the last of the historical books. In the Hebrew Scriptures it is the last of the five festival scrolls,[1] so-called because they are appointed for public reading on festival days. The feast of Purim, whose origin the book describes, comes at the end of the Jewish ecclesiastical year, about a month before Passover.

Contents of the Book of Esther

SETTING AND INTRODUCTION OF PRINCIPAL CHARACTERS (1:1–3:6)

Ahasuerus/Xerxes

In an introductory section the author brings on stage the chief characters of his highly dramatic story. He provides background information about them that the reader needs to know in order to understand their respective roles.

First to make his appearance is the Persian king, Ahasuerus (Gk.: Xerxes), because the outcome of the issues depends on his decision.

Xerxes' domestic affairs rather than his military exploits furnish the setting of the account. His rejection of one queen and selection of her successor precipitate the action and to a great extent determine the course of events.

At a banquet for the men of high office (1:1–9), the king, "merry with wine" (v. 10), ordered Queen Vashti to display "her beauty" to those in attendance. She refused to comply with his wishes (vv. 10–12). Thereupon his guests, as befuddled as he, advised him not only to depose Vashti but also to issue a pompous decree throughout the empire that "each man should be master in his own house" (vv. 13–22).

Esther

Next in the cast of characters to be introduced is the heroine, Esther. Her appearance on the scene is a natural sequel to the state of affairs created by an ill-tempered, autocratic ruler (1:1–2:4).

Before the dramatic conflict gets under way, the reader learns how this orphaned Jewish girl rose to a favored position in the royal harem (2:5–11) and then to a place at Xerxes' side as his

---

[1]The festival scrolls are Ruth, Song of Solomon, Ecclesiastes, Lamentations, and Esther.

queen[2] (vv. 12–18).

Like other exiles (cf. Dan. 1:6–7), Esther also had a Hebrew name: Hadasseh—a derivative of a common Hebrew noun meaning "myrtle." The name Esther, an adaptation of the Persian word *stareh*, means "star," a variation of the name of a goddess known in Babylonia as Ishtar and in Canaan as Ashtoreth.

Mordecai

Because Esther's parents had died, her cousin and fellow exile, Mordecai,[3] became her guardian. Both of them were in Babylonia because their common grandfather, Kish, "had been captured with Jeconiah" (also known as Jehoiachin) by Nebuchadnezzar in 597 B.C., more than a 100 years previously (2:6; cf. 2 Kings 24:8–16).

Haman

The last of the principal characters to be introduced is the villain, Haman, the grand vizier of Xerxes. Anyone who incurred this formidable opponent's displeasure would find it hard to survive. He was ruthless and cruel. "Filled with wrath" (3:5) over Mordecai's refusal to "bow or pay him homage," Haman "sought to destroy all the Jews" (vv. 1–6).

The lines of combat are drawn. Hero (2:19–23) and heroine (vv. 5–18) must match wits with a man bent on murdering an entire people (3:1–6).

Plot to Liquidate the Jews

The main action of the book is precipitated by Haman's plot to kill all Jews, not Mordecai alone. Evidently the particular act of homage required by Haman implied a violation of covenantal religious principles, and Mordecai's refusal implied that more Jews also would refuse to obey (3:7–15).

It was five years after Esther became queen (2:16) that Haman initiated his vicious program. The villain planned carefully. Before getting the king's approval, he cast lots (Pur; 3:7) to make sure what day would be auspicious for his scheme. To obtain the king's approval he had to tell a big lie; he portrayed Jews as detrimental to the state because they refused to be assimilated. Haman suggested, furthermore, that his proposal would be financially prof-

---

[2]Although secular history has no record of a Jewish queen of Xerxes, it records none of Xerxes' wives or harem except one named Amestris.

[3]The name is likely an adaptation of the common Babylonian name Mardukaia, i.e., a devotee of the god Marduk (cf. Ezra 2:2).

itable since the property of the executed "criminals" would be forfeit to the crown (vv. 7–11). Duped by his vizier, the king sent out official notices ordering that the Jews in every province be executed on the day agreed on (vv. 12–15).

COUNTERPLOT TO SAVE THE JEWS (4:4–8:17)

Drastic action was required if Haman's wicked designs were to be foiled. Mordecai promptly set in motion a counterplot by enlisting Esther's cooperation. Reluctant at first, she agreed to risk her life "to go [unbidden] in to the king to make supplication to him and plead before him for her people" (4:8). Her charm gained her an unusual audience with the king at which she invited him to a banquet in his honor.

Esther let the first day of the banquet pass (7:1) without telling the king what was so urgent that she risked an unannounced visit with him. On the second day of the banquet, when the king again pressed her for an answer, she decided she had nothing to gain if she postponed the moment of decision any longer. As straightforward as necessary and as diplomatically as possible, she presented her case.

The result was a dramatic and drastic reversal of fortunes: (1) Not Mordecai but Haman was hanged on the gallows (vv. 2–10), and (2) Haman's position of grand vizier was entrusted to his intended victim (8:1–2). The villain would no longer harm the Jews.

But the decree that Haman had masterminded "to destroy all the Jews" (3:6) was still in effect. Even the king's hands were tied; he could not, as Esther requested (8:5), "revoke the letters devised by Haman." The best the king could do was to let a proclamation go out in his name that would neutralize the effects of the original edict without canceling it (vv. 7–8).

Mordecai, the new vizier, acted at once. He issued a decree supplementing the earlier one (v. 9). The new directive authorized the condemned people to "protect their lives" (v. 11). And if in the process the Jews were "to destroy, kill, and annihilate all the forces . . . that would assault them . . . [and] plunder their possessions" (v. 11), they would not be liable under the king for murder and theft.

COUNTERMEASURES CARRIED OUT

As the tables had been turned on Haman (7:10), so the new edict effected a reversal in the fate of the Jews. Allowed "to avenge themselves on their enemies" (8:13), they got the mastery over their foes as planned. In "all the provinces" they turned on those "who hated them." In Susa alone they "killed and destroyed five hundred men" (9:6). At Esther's request the king granted the Jews in the capital even a second day on which they had a free hand to destroy their enemies (vv. 13–15). On the third day the Jews gathered in Susa for feasting and gladness (vv. 16–19).

DELIVERANCE COMMEMORATED (9:20–32)

Mordecai called on "all the Jews" to make the days on which they "had rest from their enemies" (v. 22) occasions for annual celebrations (v. 21). To confirm Mordecai's new holiday, Queen Esther lent her prestige to her cousin's ordinance (vv. 29–32).

The name that the newly ordained festival acquired (Purim) was a reminder of how close the "wicked plot" came to being successful. All that remained for "the enemy of all the Jews" and his cohorts was to await the day set for the execution—which could not fail because they had selected the date by casting what they called "Purim" (lots; cf. 3:7). At the annual commemoration of these days, the Jews were to rejoice that they were not helpless victims of a blind fate (9:23–28), and that divine providence overruled this casting of lots.

SEQUEL (10:1–3)

The book concludes with a brief sequel to the story. The Jews did not have to fear a repetition of Haman's threat to their lives for some time. They were safe everywhere, at least as long as Mordecai was the highest official of a king whose "power and . . . might" stretched "from India to Ethiopia" (1:1).

• • • • •

Epilog and Preview

The book of Esther affirms again that the Lord of heaven and earth directs world history to protect and preserve the nation through which "all the families of the earth" were to be blessed (Gen. 12:1–3). When the descendants of Abraham first seemed doomed to extinction, God rescued them from the mighty Egyptian world power, led them to safety, and made a covenant with them to be "a holy people to the LORD" (Deut. 14:2) and the bearers of His promise to redeem the world.

The book of Esther reports that a thousand years later the Israelites were again in danger of extermination. As He did at the time of the Exodus, God intervened in the affairs of a mighty empire (now centered in Persia), reversed its wicked design, and kept His covenant people alive.

Another four centuries were to elapse before the Promised Seed of Abraham appeared on the scene to redeem humanity from the threat of eternal death. In the meantime, no one was to fear that God would be frustrated by the might of men from remembering "His Holy covenant" and keeping its promises (Luke 1:72).